Mike Zollo, Alan Wesson

D0265759

spanish
grammar
made
easy

Hodder Arnold

A MEMBER OF THE HODDER HEADLINE GROUP

Orders: please contact Bookpoint Ltd, 130 Milton Park, Abingdon, Oxon
OX14 4SB. Telephone: (+44) 01235 827720. Fax (+44) 01235 400454.
Lines are open from 9.00am to 6.00pm, Monday to Saturday, with a 24-hour
message answering service. You can also order through our website
www.hoddereducation.co.uk.

If you have any comments to make about this, or any of our other titles, please
send them to educationenquiries@hodder.co.uk

British Library Cataloguing in Publication Data
A catalogue record for this title is available from the British Library

ISBN-10: 0 340 904 95X
ISBN-13: 978 0 340 904 954

First Edition Published 2005
Impression number   10 9 8 7 6 5 4 3 2 1
Year   2009 2008 2007 2006 2005

All illustrations drawn by Chris Blythe/Daedalus Studio
Typeset in 10.5/12pt New Baskerville by Servis Filmsetting Ltd, Manchester
Printed and bound in Malta for Hodder Arnold, an imprint of Hodder Education, a
member of the Hodder Headline Group, 338 Euston Road, London NW1 3BH.

CONTENTS

2 Nouns and Determiners

3 Pronouns

4 Adjectives

5 Adverbs

INTRODUCTION

Spanish Grammar Made Easy is a Spanish grammar workbook aimed at adult non-linguists, that is adults with some rudimentary knowledge of Spanish, who do not necessarily know anything about grammar, but need to learn about it so they can progress beyond phrasebook Spanish.

In the past, grammar has been seen as a barrier to language learning. It has put more people off learning a language than it has helped. Because of the way grammar has been portrayed, students were often made to feel that only those who could master 'conjugations' and 'declensions' could learn a language. In fact, you can drive a car without mastering the principles of the internal combustion engine – but if you do learn where to put the oil and how to check the tyres and fill up the windscreen wash, it does help!

Grammar is about recognising word patterns which give you a framework to a language; if you know the framework, you can 'build' new language of your own instead of having to learn everything by heart.

For those who already know some Spanish grammar, short cuts are marked with ▶▶ to enable you to go straight to the information you need. If you feel you would like to have more in-depth knowledge about a particular grammar point, please refer to *¡Acción Gramática!* or *¡Viva la Gramática!* P. Turk and M. Zollo, or to *A New Reference Grammar of Modern Spanish,* J. Butt & C. Benjamin, 1988/1994/2000/2004, 4th edn.

An interactive CD-ROM accompanies this book for use with a PC. The CD-ROM contains most of the exercises from the book as well as some additional material. Most exercises are recorded so that you can listen to a native speaker saying the sentences and there is a 'click on' facility to allow you to read the English translation. There is also some additional listening material which provides a useful resource and brings the language to life.

A simple guide to the parts of speech

▶ ▶ **If you know what verbs, nouns, pronouns, adverbs, etc. are, go on to 1.1.**

The most useful categories of words to recognise are:

1 Verbs – 'doing' words

Verbs tell you what someone or something is doing.

> I *am going* to Spain. My friend *booked* the flight. I *am going* to a meeting.

You also use them to ask questions ...

> *Have* you *seen* the film? *Are* you all right?

... and to give instructions.

> *Fetch* it! *Slow* down! *Help* me! *Wait*!

Verbs usually present the most problems, so the section dealing with them is the longest one and comes first in the book.

2 Nouns – 'naming' words

Nouns are the words which tell you:

- what something is:
  a *timetable*, a *train*, a *station*, a *town*, a *secret*
- who someone is:
  a *steward*, a *bank clerk*, a *baker*, a *student*

3 Pronouns

Pronouns are words which 'stand in' for a noun.

> Sr Morales is Spanish. Sr Morales lives in Madrid.

Instead of repeating *Sr Morales*, you can say *he*.

> Sr Morales is Spanish. *He* lives in Madrid.

In the same way, you can say *she* instead of repeating *Marisa* in the following sentence.

> Marisa works in Santander. *She* works at the ferry port.

These are also pronouns: *I, you, it, one, we, they, me, us, them.*

4 Adjectives

Adjectives are 'describing' words. They are used to describe something or someone.

the *new* house, the *red* car, a *tiny* flat, a *wet* day, a *busy* secretary

5 Adverbs

Adverbs are words which usually describe a verb, e.g. they describe how something is done. They often answer the question *How?* and in English they often end in *-ly*.

He runs *fast*. She eats *slowly*. It comes *naturally*!

6 Prepositions

Prepositions are words which usually tell you where something is, e.g. *in, under, on*. Words such as *to, for, with,* and *without* are also prepositions.

1 VERBS

1.1 Verbs: talking about what you do

▶▶ **If you know what a verb is, go on to 1.1.1.**

You use a verb to talk about what someone or something does, is doing, has done or intends to do, or what someone is being, has been or intends to be. A verb can be called a 'doing' or 'being' word.

 To find out if a word is a verb, ask yourself if someone could *do* it.

I Which of these words are things you can 'do'?

a walk
b trainers
c shout
d invent
e loud
f computer
g behind
h red
i listen
j before

Some words can be used as verbs and as nouns or adjectives, e.g. *drink* can be a drink in a cup or part of the verb *to drink*.

 Ask: Are they *doing* it? If they are, it is a verb.

II Which of the highlighted words are being used as verbs?

a Jack and Jill are to appear in a **play** at the local theatre.
b They will **play** the leading parts.
c They **work** during the day in an office.
d After **work** they go to rehearsals.
e Tonight they are having a **meeting** to discuss the production.
f They are **meeting** in the theatre bar.
g They need to discuss **finances**.
h A local sponsor usually **finances** the productions.

i The producer **reports** that this time there will be no sponsorship.
j According to newspaper **reports** the sponsors have gone bankrupt.

1.1.1 What is the infinitive?

▶▶ **If you know what the infinitive is, go on to 1.1.2.**

When you look up a verb in a dictionary, you will find the infinitive form of it listed first. This is the 'name' of the verb.

In English, the infinitive consists of *to* + verb, e.g. *to eat, to build, to paint.*

The infinitive is often used in Spanish to give commands, for example on public notices, especially when telling people not to do something:

Abrir con cuidado. Open carefully.
¡No pisar la hierba! Don't walk on the grass!

Below are some Spanish infinitives. You probably know some of them already or can guess what they mean.

> Try to look for similarities between the Spanish and the English. Some are obvious: for example, **organizar** means *to organise*. Others are less obvious, such as **viajar**, which means *to travel* (or *to go on a voyage*); another is **examinar**, meaning *to look at/check*, both similar to *examine*, which is of course another meaning for this verb. Don't be afraid to try out these little 'leaps of faith', thinking around the areas of possible meaning: your guesses will usually be correct.

I See how many of these Spanish infinitives you can match up with their English counterparts.

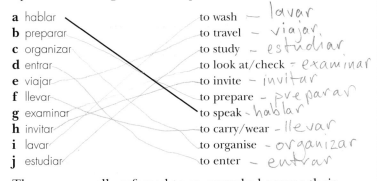

a hablar — to speak - hablar
b preparar — to prepare - preparar
c organizar — to organise - organizar
d entrar — to enter - entrar
e viajar — to travel - viajar
f llevar — to carry/wear - llevar
g examinar — to look at/check - examinar
h invitar — to invite - invitar
i lavar — to wash - lavar
j estudiar — to study - estudiar

to wash — lavar / to travel — viajar / to study — estudiar / to look at/check — examinar / to invite — invitar / to prepare — preparar / to speak — hablar / to carry/wear — llevar / to organise — organizar / to enter — entrar

Check these

These are usually referred to as **-ar** verbs because their infinitive form ends in **-ar**.

II Here are some more **-ar** verbs to match up. How many of them do you know already? They all have to do with food and eating.

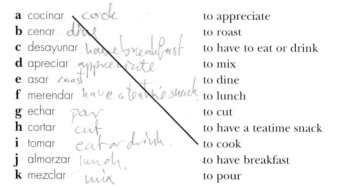

a cocinar *cook*   to appreciate
b cenar *dine*   to roast
c desayunar *have breakfast*   to have to eat or drink
d apreciar *appreciate*   to mix
e asar *roast*   to dine
f merendar *have a teatime snack*   to lunch
g echar *pour*   to cut
h cortar *cut*   to have a teatime snack
i tomar *eat or drink.*   to cook
j almorzar *lunch,*   to have breakfast
k mezclar *mix*   to pour

 If you find it difficult to learn new words, try to find a 'hook' to hang them on: e.g. **cocinar** is based on **cocina** – *kitchen*, which is like *cuisine* in French. Similarly, if you know **corto** – *short*, you can work out for yourself that **cortar** must mean *to cut*, i.e. 'to make short'.

 More than 50% of English words derive from Latin, as do more than 90% of Spanish words. Of course this means that if you don't know a verb, you can just say the English verb with a Spanish accent: you have a 50% chance of being understood.

III What do you think the Spanish for these verbs would be? Cover up the Spanish and see if you can work it out, or join the correct pairs with a line.

a to begin *comenzar*   terminar
b to accept *aceptar*   evaluar
c to separate *separar*   publicar
d to evaluate *evaluar*   navegar
e to steal *robar*   girar
f to sail *navegar*   comenzar
g to publish *publicar*   separar
h to turn (round) *girar*   robar
i to continue *continuar*   continuar
j to finish/end *terminar*   aceptar

Most verbs based on a noun or an adjective, and most of those based on words 'imported' from other languages, are **-ar** verbs:

desayuno	breakfast	desayunar	to have breakfast
escaso	rare	escasear	to be rare/become rare
chutar	to shoot	faxear	to fax

1.1.2 Groups of verbs

group 1: -ar verbs	group 2: -er verbs	group 3: -ir verbs
comprar hablar	beber comer	vivir escribir

▶▶ **If you know how to find the 'stem' or 'root' of a verb, go on to 1.1.3.**

In English, we just have regular and irregular verbs. A verb like *to dance* is regular: *dance, dances, danced, danced,* and a verb like *to fly* is irregular: *fly, flies, flew, flown.* As you have probably already noticed, Spanish verbs are more complicated! Spanish schoolchildren have to spend years learning all about Spanish verbs, but we can find some shortcuts. Spanish also has regular and irregular verbs, but we usually divide Spanish regular verbs into three main groups to make them easier to learn, depending on whether the infinitive ends in (1) **-ar**, (2) **-er** or (3) **-ir**.

The stem, or root, of the verb is the part which is left after you take off the ending. It is used in making the other forms of the verb which you use to talk about the past and the future.

I Which group do these verbs belong to, and what is their stem? (Remember: take off the **-ar**, **-er** or **-ir** to find the stem.)

a	vender	to sell	(2/vend)
b	mostrar	to show	....
c	cantar	to sing	....
d	salir	to go out	....
e	lavar	to wash	....
f	acabar	to end	....
g	escuchar	to listen	....
h	cerrar	to close/shut	....
i	dejar	to leave (behind)	....
j	coger	to take	....
k	escoger	to choose	....

l	llevar	to carry, wear	....
m	regresar	to return (home)	....
n	venir	to come	....
o	dormir	to sleep	....

Fortunately, over 80% of Spanish verbs belong to group 1 (**-ar** verbs) and they are mostly regular. When we say they are regular, we mean they follow the same pattern, so if you learn one, you can work out the endings you need for all the others.

1.1.3 Irregular verbs

Some verbs are awkward and don't really fit into any pattern. They are called 'irregular' verbs. This means that you have to learn them separately and, of course, they are the verbs you are likely to want to use most. Fortunately, you probably know quite a lot of them already, although you might not be aware of it: for example, you probably know that *I know* is **(yo) sé** or *I don't know* is **(yo) no sé** but you may not know that the infinitive is **saber**.

Note that in Spanish the person word (**yo** – *I*, etc.) is only used when emphasis or clarification is needed, because the different verb endings for each person are clear and distinctive in both speech and writing.

These are the most important irregular verbs to learn, because they are the most used:

infinitive:

ser – to be*   estar – to be*   tener – to have   ir – to go

yo form:

soy – I am   estoy – I am   tengo – I have   voy – I am going

(*For the different uses of **ser** and **estar** see 1.8.1.)

Some verbs just have an irregular *yo* form (see 1.2.2 D). Others containing an **-e-** or **-o-** have a spelling change in some forms (see sections on stem-changing verbs in 1.2.2–4 and 1.2.7).

Some verbs with an irregular **yo** form:

hacer	to do/make	hago	I do/make
coger	to take	cojo	I take
conocer	to know (a person)	conozco	I know
dar	to give	doy	I give

Some verbs with stem changes:

cerrar	to close	cierro	I close
querer	to want	quiero	I want
preferir	to prefer	prefiero	I prefer
probar	to try on	pruebo	I try on
volver	to return	vuelvo	I return
dormir	to sleep	duermo	I sleep

Note also that verbs based on an irregular verb follow the same irregular pattern, for example:

hacer – to make/do → deshacer – to undo/take to pieces

tener – to have → retener – to retain

coger – to take → escoger – to choose

probar – to try on → aprobar – to approve

Always look for patterns which will help you to remember new words, e.g.

reír – to laugh → sonreír – to smile

I Match the infinitives.

a to know how to — poder – to be able to

b to see — ir to go

c to have — ser to be

d to go — saber to know – you learnt ?

e to be able to — deber – to have to

f to have to — hacer – to do

g to want to — querer – to want to

h to take — tener — to have

i to be — coger – to take

j to do — ver – to see

1.1.4 The 'persons' of the verb

▶ ▶ **If you know about the 'persons' of the verb, go on to 1.1.5.**

- When we talk about ourselves, it is called the 'first person'.
- When we talk about or to *you*, it is called the 'second person'.
- When we talk about someone else, it is called the 'third person'.

Note that in Spanish the formal forms of *you*, **usted** and **ustedes**, use the third person verbs.

In English, we only change the ending when we are talking about *he*, *she* or *it*:

	singular	**plural**
first person	I talk	we talk
second person	you talk	you talk
third person	he/she/it talks	they talk

In many languages, including Spanish, the verb ending changes according to who is doing the action and you have to learn the pattern of the verb. In Spanish, the ending changes in clear patterns to show who is doing the action.

Fortunately, in Spanish not only are the endings spelt differently, they all sound different, so there is never any confusion about who is doing what. This is why the 'person words' are usually not needed.

	singular	**plural**
first person	(yo) hablo	(nosotros) hablamos
second person	(tú) hablas	(vosotros) habláis
third person	(él/ella/usted) habla	(ellos/ellas/ustedes) hablan

I	yo
you (familiar singular)	tú
he	él
she	ella
you (formal singular)	usted
we (my friend and I)	nosotros/as
you (familiar plural)	vosotros/as
they	ellos
they (if they are all female)	ellas
you (formal plural)	ustedes

Yo, **tú**, **él**, **ella**, etc. are called pronouns because they 'stand in' for, or represent, a person or thing: Mr Smith – *he*; Mr and Mrs Smith – *they*; Jim Smith and I – *we*, etc.

The **tú** form is only used when talking to a child, a relation or a very good friend. It implies a certain degree of intimacy and should not be used to address an adult unless he or she invites you to use it (see 1.2.3), although in many parts of Spain people of your age will use it in addressing you – so you can use it to them. **Usted** is used for formal situations.

The same is true in the plural with **vosotros/as** and **ustedes**. Note that **usted** and **ustedes** use the third person verb forms (*he/she* and *they* respectively).

Nosotros/as and **vosotros/as** have masculine and feminine forms, but you can only use the feminine form if all the people concerned are female.

Él/Ella – *he/she*: there is no word for *it* as everything in Spanish is either masculine or feminine: even a table and chair are feminine words.

Ellos is used for a group of male people (or things) or a group that includes one or more males, even if there are more females than males present. **Ellas** is only used for a group of all female people or things.

▶▶ **For more information on pronouns, go on to 3.1.**

I   Which pronoun would you use?

a You are talking about yourself: tú/yo/él
   I am speaking.
b You are talking about a girlfriend.   yo/vosotros/ella
c You are talking about a male friend.   nosotros/él/ella
d You are talking about yourself   él/ella/nosotros
   and a male friend.
e You are talking to two little girls.   tú/vosotros/vosotras
f You are talking to a stranger.   usted/vosotros/tú
g You are talking about a group   ellos/ella/ellas
   of women.
h You are talking about a mixed group   ellos/ustedes/él
   or a group of men.

II   And which pronoun would you use when talking about the following people?

a your friend Pablo   nosotros/él/ella
b your friend María   ellas/ella/tú
c Señor Blanco   vosotros/usted/él
d Señor y señora Lafuente   ellos/ellas/ustedes
e Señoras Blanco y Botella   ellas/ellos/nosotras
f Silvia y Carlota   ellos/ellas/vosotras
g yourself   tú/vosotros/yo
h Pablo, Guillermo y María   ellos/vosotros/ellas
i Señores Múgica, Barranco y Durán   nosotros/vosotros/ellos
j yourself and your male friend   nosotros/vosotras/yo

1.1.5 ▶Fast track: Verbs

Verbs are 'doing' words: you use them to say what you (or someone/something else) are doing and to ask someone what he/she is doing.

In English, when we look up a verb in the dictionary it is preceded by the word *to*: *to go*; *to drive*; *to eat*, etc. This is called the infinitive.

In Spanish, the infinitive is visible by its last two letters, so it is the *end* of the verb which is important. All Spanish infinitives end in **-ar**, **-er** or **-ir**. Each of these is a sort of 'last name' for a large family of verbs which share their behaviour and characteristics.

In English, we just have two main sorts of verbs: regular and irregular.

In Spanish, there are three main groups or families of verbs:

-ar verbs which are regular and **-ar** verbs which are irregular
-er verbs which are regular and **-er** verbs which are irregular
-ir verbs which are regular and **-ir** verbs which are irregular.

In English, regular and irregular verbs change the ending when talking about *he/she/it*:

I speak → he speaks   I go → she goes   I fly → it flies

In Spanish, the verb ending changes for all the different people.

The different persons are:

singular		plural	
I	yo	we	nosotros/as
you (familiar)	tú	you (familiar)	vosotros/as
he/she/it	él/ella	they	ellos/ellas
you (formal)	usted	you (formal)	ustedes

1.2 Talking about what you are doing now: the present tense

▶▶ **If you know about the present tense and when to use it, go on to 1.2.8.**

The present tense is used

- to say what you are doing now: *I am reading.*
- to make a general statement about what happens: *It often rains in northern Spain.*
- to say what usually happens: *We go out on Friday evenings.*
- to talk about something which will happen soon: *Mum arrives on the 7 o'clock train.*

In English, we have two ways of talking about the present. We can either use *am, is* or *are* to say what we are doing now ...

I am working.
My friends are going out.
It is raining.

... or we can say what usually/generally happens, using the verb without the *am, is* or *are*:

I read magazines.
They are vegetarian.
It rains every day.

In Spanish, there are the same two ways of expressing the present tense, but the simple one-word form is enough to describe something going on at present unless you want to emphasise the fact that something is happening right now, in which case the longer form is used. (See 1.2.1.)

Leo el periódico.	I read/I am reading the newspaper.
Trabajan en el aeropuerto.	They work/They are working at the airport.
Sr López coge el autobús.	Mr López is taking/takes the bus.

I Find the right verb in the box to say these things in Spanish.

acompañar, cenar, descargar, estudiar, ir, prestar, recoger, telefonear, visitar, volar

a I am downloading my e-mails.
b My friend is ringing me when she gets home.
c She is accompanying her parents to the airport.
d We are going to the cinema later.
e She is fetching me.
f Her parents are lending her their car.
g They are flying to Buenos Aires.
h They are visiting their other daughter.
i She is studying in Argentina.
j After the cinema we are dining at the Restaurante de la Plata.

1.2.1 Talking about what you are doing at this moment: the present continuous tense

▶▶ **If you know about the present continuous tense and when to use it, go on to 1.2.8.**

As mentioned above, Spanish has a direct equivalent of the English present with *am/is/are*, which is known as the present continuous tense. The appropriate part of the verb **estar** in the present tense is used with a part of the main verb which is equivalent to English *-ing*. This is called the gerund (sometimes also known as the present participle). For **-ar** verbs, the gerund ends in **-ando**, and for **-er** and **-ir** verbs it ends in **-iendo**.

I Here are examples of the present continuous for each person of the verb. Can you translate them?

a estoy cantando
b estás comiendo
c está bebiendo
d estamos trabajando
e estáis viajando
f están subiendo

There are a few verbs with slightly irregular *-ing* forms which can be learnt easily.

Remember, this form is not used as much in Spanish as it is in English. The normal present is usually enough.

1.2.2 Talking about yourself: *yo*

Remember, in Spanish the verb ending changes according to who is doing the action.

▶▶ **If you know about the yo form, go to the checklist on page 23.**

A   Yo and regular **-ar** verbs

These are verbs which end in **-ar** in the infinitive.

The infinitive is the form you find in the dictionary when you look up a verb.

 Over 80% of Spanish verbs end in **-ar** and are regular.

In the **yo** form (or first person) of the present tense, all **-ar** verbs end in **-o**. Try reading the 'first person' column aloud.

infinitive	meaning	first person	meaning
escuchar	to listen	escucho	I listen
explicar	to explain	explico	I explain
hablar	to speak	hablo	I speak
llegar	to arrive	llego	I arrive
llevar	to carry/wear	llevo	I carry/wear
mirar	to look at/watch	miro	I look at/watch
tocar	to touch/play (an instrument)	toco	I touch/play
tomar	to take	tomo	I take
trabajar	to work	trabajo	I work
visitar	to visit	visito	I visit

Remember that all these Spanish forms can also translate *am ...ing*, and that it is not necessary to translate *am* from English into Spanish unless you use the present continuous for emphasis. (See 1.2.1.)

 The **yo** form of all **-ar** verbs ends in **-o** except for **estar** – **estoy** and **dar** – **doy**.

I   How would you say these in Spanish? Remember, **yo** is only needed for clarification or emphasis.

a I speak English.   Yo _____ inglés.
b I have tea to drink.   _____ té.
c I am wearing jeans.   _____ unos vaqueros.
d I work in an office.   _____ en una oficina.
e I am listening to the news.   _____ las noticias.
f I play the guitar.   _____ la guitarra.
g I visit the town.   _____ el pueblo.
h I am watching the children.   _____ a los niños.
i I am arriving home.   _____ a casa.
j I am explaining the firm's   _____ la política de
       policies.   la empresa.

II These are all **-ar** verbs. Fill in the gaps.

a _____ en una oficina. (trabajar)   I work in an office.
b _____ a las ocho. (llegar)   I arrive at 8 o'clock.
c _____ mi coche. (aparcar)   I park my car.
d _____ en el edificio. (entrar)   I enter the building.
e _____ al conserje. (saludar)   I greet the caretaker.
f _____ el ascensor al cuarto   I take the lift to the fourth floor.
piso. (tomar)

g _____ las llaves en mi bolsillo.   I look for my keys in my pocket.
(buscar)

h _____ en mi despacho. (entrar)   I go into my office.
i _____ mis papeles de mi cartera.   I take my papers out of my
(sacar)   briefcase.

j _____ hasta las doce. (trabajar)   I work until twelve.

Now cover up the left-hand side of the page and see if you
can do them again. Say them aloud!

Choose five of the verbs which you didn't know before (or had
forgotten) and which you think would be useful to learn. Write
down the meaning and the first letter of the verb. See how many
you can remember.

III How would you say the following?

a I am going into the shop.   Yo _____ en la tienda. (entrar)
b I am buying a new car.   _____ un coche nuevo. (comprar)
c I am calling my secretary.   _____ a mi secretaria. (llamar)
d I'll have a beer.   _____ una cerveza. (tomar)
e I'm paying.   Yo _____. (pagar)
f I am sending a letter.   _____ una carta. (enviar)
g I hope the weather will be   _____ que haga buen tiempo.
fine.   (esperar)

h I am trying to answer the   _____ de contestar a la pregunta.
question.   (tratar)

i I am throwing out the old   _____ los viejos diarios a la
papers.   basura. (echar)

j I congratulate you!   ¡Te _____ ! (felicitar)

Highlight any verbs which you think would be useful for you to use
some time.

Remember, the overwhelming majority of **-ar** verbs are regular.
The **yo** forms of all but two **-ar** verbs (**estar** and **dar**: see
section D) end in **-o**.

IV Complete these sentences with the right form of the verb in brackets and read them aloud.

a Yo ____ inglés. (hablar)
b ____ a Londres. (viajar)
c Me ___ una noche en Madrid. (quedar)
d ____ a un taxi. (llamar)
e ____a la estación. (llegar)
f ____ en el despacho de billetes. (entrar)
g ____ un billete para el AVE. (comprar)
h ____ el tren. (esperar)
i ____ en el vagón restaurante. (cenar)
j ____ un fax. (mandar)
k ____ con mi vecino. (charlar)
l ____un café. (tomar)
m____ a mi mejor amigo. (telefonear)
n ____el campo que pasa a 360 km/h. (mirar)

B *Yo* and regular **-er** verbs
These are verbs which end in **-er** in the infinitive.

Remember, most verbs are **-ar** verbs, so there aren't so many of these.

In the **yo** form (or first person) of the present tense, all **-er** verbs end in **-o** except for **ser – soy** and **saber – sé**. Try reading them aloud.

infinitive	meaning	first person	meaning
aprender	to learn	aprendo	I learn
beber	to drink	bebo	I drink
comer	to eat	como	I eat
comprender	to understand	comprendo	I understand
correr	to run	corro	I run
creer	to believe/ think	creo	I believe/think
leer	to read	leo	I read
proceder	to proceed	procedo	I proceed
responder	to reply	respondo	I reply
vender	to sell	vendo	I sell

V Which of the above verbs would you use?

  a You have to drink this medicine.
  b He has to eat his meal.
  c She has to run.
  d He has to respond.
  e You have to sell your house.
  f We have to read this book.
  g You must understand.
  h You have to proceed with care.
  i You have to try to learn Spanish grammar!
  j Don't believe that!

VI Match the English and the Spanish.

  a I drink/am drinking *bebo*   vendo
  b I eat/am eating *como*   procedo
  c I run/am running *corro*   aprendo
  d I read/am reading *leo*   comprendo
  e I sell/am selling *vendo*   bebo
  f I learn/am learning *aprendo*   corro
  g I proceed/am proceeding *procedo*   respondo
  h I believe *creo*   como
  i I understand *comprendo*   leo
  j I am responding *respondo*   creo

Some **-er** verbs have a special spelling and pronunciation change in the **yo** form to 'reinforce' their sound (see section D). The most useful ones are **hacer**, **traer**, **tener**, **poner**, **saber** and **conocer**.

C *Yo* and regular **-ir** verbs

These are verbs which end in **-ir** in the infinitive.

Remember, most verbs are **-ar** verbs, so there aren't many of these.

Like almost all verbs in the present tense, these end in **-o** when you are talking about yourself (in the first person singular). The only exception is **ir**, which has the form **voy**. Practise saying them aloud, as it will help you to remember them.

infinitive	meaning	first person	meaning
asistir	to attend	asisto	I attend
describir	to describe	describo	I describe
dividir	to divide	divido	I divide
escribir	to write	escribo	I write
recibir	to receive	recibo	I receive
subir	to go up	subo	I go up
sufrir	to suffer	sufro	I suffer
vivir	to live	vivo	I live

VII   How would you say the following?

a I am living at my parents' home.   _____ en casa de mis padres. (vivir)

b I am going upstairs.   _____ arriba. (subir)

c I am suffering from an injustice.   _____ una injusticia. (sufrir)

d I am writing a letter.   _____ una carta. (escribir)

e I am describing my friend.   _____ a mi amigo. (describir)

f I divide my time carefully.   _____ mi tiempo con cuidado. (dividir)

g I receive lots of e-mail messages.   _____ mucho correo electrónico. (recibir)

h I go to mass here on Sundays.   _____ a la misa aquí los domingos. (asistir)

Now cover up the right-hand side of the page and see if you can still do them.

infinitive	meaning	first person	meaning
abrir	to open	abro	I open
admitir	to admit	admito	I admit
cubrir	to cover	cubro	I cover
decidir	to decide	decido	I decide
descubrir	to discover	descubro	I discover
discutir	to discuss	discuto	I discuss
persuadir	to persuade	persuado	I persuade
sobrevivir	to survive	sobrevivo	I survive

VIII   How would you say the following?

a I am going up.   Yo _____. (subir)

b I live in Granada.   _____ en Granada. (vivir)

c I am deciding today.   _____ hoy. (decidir)

d I am attending the wedding.   _____ a la boda. (asistir)

e I am discussing the matter.   _____ la cuestión. (discutir)

f I suffer every day.   _____ todos los días. (sufrir)

g I persuade my friends.   _____ a mis amigos. (persuadir)

h I accept that I am wrong. _____ que estoy equivocado.
(admitir)

i I divide up the cake. _____ el pastel. (dividir)

j I survive – just! _____ ¡apenas! (sobrevivir)

Now cover up the right-hand side of the page and see if you can still do them.

IX How would you say the following?

a I am discussing the news. _____ las noticias. (discutir)

b I am going up in the lift. _____ en el ascensor. (subir)

c I discover the truth. _____ la verdad. (descubrir)

d I am dividing up this money. _____ este dinero. (dividir)

e I am covering the baby. _____ al bebé. (cubrir)

f I am opening the window. _____ la ventana. (abrir)

> Say the verbs aloud to get used to the sound of the words: which ones sound a little like the English?

D Verbs which change their spelling in the *yo* form

Some verbs in each of the three verb families modify their spelling and pronunciation in the first person singular. This is to make the verb easier to pronounce or to give it a stronger sound. Apart from the first five in the list below, they all still end in **-o** as you would expect.

Here are the most useful examples:

ser – soy	I am
estar – estoy	I am (See 1.8.1 on **ser** and **estar**)
dar – doy	I give
ir – voy	I go
saber – sé	I know (a fact)
decir – digo	I say
oír – oigo	I hear
hacer – hago	I do
traer – traigo	I bring
tener – tengo	I have
venir – vengo	I come
poner – pongo	I put
salir – salgo	I go out
conocer – conozco	I know (a person, a place)
conducir – conduzco	I drive
ver – veo	I see

X   How would you say the following?

a I have a brother.	_____ un hermano. (tener)
b I have to go.	_____ que irme. (tener)
c I know!	¡Ya lo _____! (saber)
d I put it on the table.	Lo _____ en la mesa. (poner)
e I go out often.	_____ con frecuencia. (salir)
f I know that girl.	_____ a esa chica. (conocer)
g I say this every day.	Lo _____ todos los días. (decir)
h I can speak Italian.	_____ hablar italiano. (saber)
i I am giving her a new car.	Le _____ un coche nuevo. (dar)

Cover up the Spanish. Can you still do them?

E   *Yo and verbs which change their stem*

Some verbs in each of the three main families modify their stem in the first person. This is to make the verb sound stronger by 'stretching' the vowel from -e- to -ie-, or -o- to -ue-. A few have -e- to -i-, and just one has a change from -u- to -ue-.

Here are the most useful examples:

stem change	infinitive	meaning	first person	meaning
e → ie	p**e**nsar	to think	p**ie**nso	I think
	qu**e**rer	to want	qu**ie**ro	I want
	pref**e**rir	to prefer	pref**ie**ro	I prefer
o → ue	c**o**ntar	to count	c**ue**nto	I count
	v**o**lver	to return	v**ue**lvo	I return
	d**o**rmir	to sleep	d**ue**rmo	I sleep
e → i	p**e**dir	to ask for	p**i**do	I ask for
u → ue	j**u**gar	to play	j**ue**go	I play

XI   Choose a verb from the list above and complete each sentence with the correct form.

a I want to play tennis.	_____ jugar al tenis.
b I think my girlfriend has a racket.	_____ que mi novia tiene una raqueta.
c I ask for her racket.	Le _____ su raqueta.
d I am counting on her.	_____ con ella.
e I play tennis with you.	_____ al tenis contigo.
f I prefer to win!	¡_____ ganar!
g I go home afterwards.	Después _____ a casa.
h Then I sleep very well.	Luego _____ muy bien.

F   Yo and reflexive verbs

▶▶ **If you know about reflexive verbs, go on to the checklist on page 23.**

We don't have an equivalent form in English, but you probably already know the reflexive verb **llamarse** *to be called*. **Me llamo** means *I am called* or literally *I call myself*. The infinitive is **llamarse**. Notice how the reflexive 'self' word is stuck onto the end of the infinitive.

When using a specific part of one of these verbs, start with the appropriate 'self' word: when you are talking about yourself, you use **me** and the first person of the verb, just as normal.

There are more reflexive verbs in Spanish than in English, many of which are not expressed with 'self' in English. Notice how most of the following have the idea of doing something to yourself:

infinitive	meaning	first person	meaning
aburrirse	to get bored	me aburro	I get bored
acostarse	to go to bed	me acuesto	I go to bed
despertarse	to wake up	me despierto	I wake up
ducharse	to have a shower	me ducho	I have a shower
lavarse	to wash (oneself)	me lavo	I wash (myself)
levantarse	to get up	me levanto	I get up
llamarse	to be called	me llamo	I am called
pelearse	to quarrel	me peleo	I quarrel
preguntarse	to wonder	me pregunto	I wonder
sentarse	to sit down	me siento	I sit down
vestirse	to get dressed	me visto	I get dressed

XII   How would you say the following?

a I wake up at seven o'clock. _____ a las siete.
b I get up straight away. _____ en seguida.
c I am washing my hair. _____ el pelo.
d I am having a shower. _____
e I get dressed. _____
f I sit down. _____
g I wonder whether the taxi has arrived already. _____ si el taxi ya ha llegado.
h I am getting bored. _____
i I quarrel with my friend. _____ con mi amigo.
j I am going to bed. _____

G Saying you like something

Spanish does not really have a verb for *to like*. Instead, it uses *to please* as a sort of 'back-to-front' way of conveying the idea of liking: **me gusta esta casa** literally means *this house pleases me*.

To say you like more than one thing, the verb adds **-n**: **me gustan estas casas**.

Note that the verb agrees with the *thing liked*, which is the subject. The person liking is expressed by a pronoun. There are other expressions which work like this; here is a list of the most useful ones:

verb	I ... (singular)	I ... (plural)	meaning
gustar	me gusta	me gustan	I like ...
encantar	me encanta	me encantan	I like ... a lot, love ...
interesar	me interesa	me interesan	I am interested in ...
apetecer	me apetece	me apetecen	I feel like ...
quedar	me queda	me quedan	I have ... left
doler	me duele	me duelen	my ... hurt(s)
hacer falta	me hace falta	me hacen falta	I need ...

XIII Say that ...

a ... your head hurts   _____ la cabeza.

b ... you need some aspirin   _____ aspirina.

c ... you only have two left   Sólo _____ dos.

d ... you like soluble aspirins   _____ las aspirinas solubles.

e ... you feel like watching television   _____ ver la televisión.

f ... you love soap operas   _____ las telenovelas.

g ... you are interested in the characters   _____ los personajes.

Checklist: the yo form

- When talking about yourself in the present tense, you use **yo** (but only when necessary) and the first person singular of the verb.
- To form the first person singular of the verb, you take off the **-ar/-er/-ir** ending.
- You then add **-o**.
- The most important irregular **yo** forms to remember are:
  ser – to be → soy – I am (quality, characteristic, profession, etc.)
  estar – to be → estoy – I am (place or state)
  tener – to have → tengo – I have
  ir – to go → voy – I go
  hacer – to do → hago – I do

• Check you know these other useful irregular verbs:
saber – to know → sé – I know (how to do something)
conocer – to know → conozco – I know (a person or place)
venir – to come → vengo – I come/am coming

1.2.3 Talking to someone younger or someone you know well: *tú*

This is the *you* form, or the second person of the verb.

There are actually four forms of *you* in Spanish: the familiar forms **tú** (singular) and **vosotros/as** (plural) and the formal forms **usted** (singular) and **ustedes** (plural).

You use the **tú** form if you are talking to someone you know well – a friend, a child or a pet. You do not use it to a stranger, a business acquaintance or an older person unless invited to do so.

There is a special verb which means to call someone **tú**: **tutear**. If someone says: **Podemos tutearnos, ¿verdad?** it means 'let's use the **tú** form'.

> The **tú** form is easy, as in all verbs in the present tense, and in many other tenses, it ends in **-as** or **-es**.

▶▶ **If you are not going to need the tú form, go on to 1.2.4.**

A *Tú* and regular verbs

-ar verbs

The **tú** form is formed by adding **-as** to the stem of the verb; remember that in Spanish all letters are pronounced except for **h** (never pronounced), so these endings are very clear and distinct, which is why the **tú** itself is not normally needed in front of the verb:

(yo) hablo, (tú) hablas

-er and -ir verbs

The **tú** form is formed by adding **-es** to the stem:

(yo) como, (tú) comes
(yo) vivo, (tú) vives

I   What is the **tú** form of these verbs?

a dance	**f** eat
b drink	**g** listen
c live	**h** write
d speak	**i** wash
e watch	**j** work

B   *Tú and irregular verbs*

some of the most common and useful verbs are irregular in the **tú** form.

infinitive	meaning	second person	meaning
estar	to be	estás	you are
ser	to be	eres	you are
ir	to go	vas	you go

C   *Tú and stem-changing verbs*

The verbs which modify the spelling of their stem in the first person do the same with **tú**. Thus, the 'stretching' vowel **-e-** changes to **-ie-**, and **-o-** to **-ue-**. As before, a few have **-e-** to **-i-**, and just one has a change from **-u-** to **-ue-**.

Here are the most useful examples:

stem change	infinitive	meaning	third person	meaning
e → ie	pensar	to think	piensas	you think
	querer	to want	quieres	you want
	preferir	to prefer	prefieres	you prefer
o → ue	contar	to count	cuentas	you count
	volver	to return	vuelves	you return
	dormir	to sleep	duermes	you sleep
e → i	pedir	to ask for	pides	you ask for
u → ue	jugar	to play	juegas	you play

Note that **tener** is another of these verbs: the **tú** form is **tienes**.

II   Choose a verb from the list above and complete each sentence or question with the correct form. Then, if you are feeling adventurous, translate them into English!

a ¿____ jugar al tenis conmigo?

b ¿____ que vas a ganar?

c Le _____ una raqueta a tu amigo.
d _____ con él, es muy generoso.
e _____ al tenis conmigo.
f ¡_____ ganar, pero es imposible!
g Después _____ a casa.
h Luego _____ muy bien.

III Use the right form of the verbs in brackets to tell someone what they are like.

a You are talkative. — (Tú) _____ hablador(a). (ser)
b You have got a spot on your nose. — _____ un grano en la nariz. (tener)
c You go to the swimming pool. — _____ a la piscina. (ir)
d You eat pizzas. — _____ pizzas. (comer)
e You watch soaps. — _____ las telenovelas. (ver)
f You live in Barcelona. — _____ en Barcelona. (vivir)
g You speak English. — _____ inglés. (hablar)
h You wear jeans. — _____ unos vaqueros. (llevar)
i You do sport. — _____ deporte. (hacer)
j You play tennis. — _____ al tenis. (jugar)

D *Tú* and reflexive verbs

The **tú** form follows the same pattern as the **yo** form but the reflexive pronoun is **te** instead of **me**.

infinitive	meaning	second person	meaning
aburrirse	to get bored	te aburres	you get bored
acostarse	to go to bed	te acuestas	you go to bed
despertarse	to wake up	te despiertas	you wake up
ducharse	to have a shower	te duchas	you have a shower
lavarse	to wash (oneself)	te lavas	you wash (yourself)
levantarse	to get up	te levantas	you get up
llamarse	to be called	te llamas	you are called
pelearse	to quarrel	te peleas	you quarrel
preguntarse	to wonder	te preguntas	you wonder
sentarse	to sit down	te sientas	you sit down
vestirse	to get dressed	te vistes	you get dressed

IV Match the questions. How would you ask a child ...

a his or her name?
b at what time he/she gets up?
c when he/she goes to bed?
d if he/she quarrels with his/her brother?

i ¿No te interesas por la actualidad?
ii ¿Cómo te llamas?
iii ¿Te peleas con tu hermano?
iv ¿A qué hora te levantas?

e if he/she is not interested in current affairs?

v ¿A qué hora te acuestas?

E Asking a friend or relative if he/she likes something

As we have seen, Spanish uses *to please* as a sort of 'back-to-front' way of conveying the idea of liking. To ask a friend or relative if he/she likes something, use **¿te gusta esta casa?** which literally means *does this house please you?*

To ask if he/she likes more than one thing, the verb adds **-n: ¿te gustan estas casas?**

There are other expressions which work like this; here is a list of the most useful ones:

verb	do you ... (singular)	do you ... (plural)	meaning
gustar	¿te gusta?	¿te gustan?	do you like ...?
encantar	¿te encanta?	¿te encantan?	do you like ... a lot?
interesar	¿te interesa?	¿te interesan?	are you interested in ...?
apetecer	¿te apetece?	¿te apetecen?	do you feel like ...?
quedar	¿te queda?	¿te quedan?	do you have ... left?
doler	¿te duele?	¿te duelen?	do(es) your ... hurt?
hacer falta	¿te hace falta?	¿te hacen falta?	do you need ...?

V Ask if ...

a ... your friend's feet ache   ¿_____ los pies?
b ... he/she needs some plasters   ¿_____ tiritas?
c ... he/she has any left   ¿_____ tiritas?
d ... he/she likes running   ¿_____ correr?
e ... he/she feels like going to the cinema ¿_____ ir al cine?
f ... he/she likes Almodóvar's films a lot   ¿_____ las películas de Almodóvar?
g ... he/she is interested in the actors   ¿_____ los actores?

F *Tú* and asking questions

To make a question in Spanish, you change the intonation by making your voice rise towards the end of the sentence:

¿Estás cansado?	Are you tired?
¿Te descansas?	Are you having a rest?
¿Te interesa el fútbol?	Are you interested in football?
¿Recuerdas el día cuando ...?	Do you remember the day when ...?

You can also make a question by changing the order, putting the verb first and then the subject pronoun **tú**; of course this is not done often because **tú** is not usually needed.

¿Vives tú en Madrid?	Do you live/Are you living in Madrid?
¿Juegas tú al tenis?	Do you play/Are you playing tennis?
¿Prefieres tú ir al cine?	Do you prefer to go to the cinema?
¿Escuchas tú las noticias?	Do you listen/Are you listening to the news?
¿Oyes tú bien?	Do/Can you hear well?

> Practise saying questions to get used to the sound. Remember to make your voice rise towards the end. You will probably feel silly at first, but don't worry, practice eventually makes perfect!

VI Practise asking your friend what he/she is going to do. Just add the **tú** form of the verb in brackets.

a Have you got a meeting in Madrid next Tuesday?
¿_____ una reunión en Madrid el martes que viene? (tener)

b Are you leaving very early?
¿_____ muy temprano? (salir)

c Are you taking the AVE?
¿_____ el AVE? (coger)

d Do you get in to Atocha?
¿_____ a Atocha? (llegar)

e Will you eat with us?
¿_____ con nosotros? (cenar)

f Are you going back to Seville the same evening?
¿_____ a Sevilla esa misma tarde? (volver)

VII Chatting up – imagine you have already got to the **tú** stage with somebody of the opposite sex! Match the questions, then cover the right-hand side of the page and see if you can remember the Spanish translations.

a Would you like a drink?
i ¿Quieres un cigarrillo?

b Do you prefer red or white wine?
ii ¿Estás cansado/a?

c Do you smoke?
iii ¿Quieres algo de beber?

d Do you mind if I smoke?
iv ¿Quieres ir a cenar en un restaurante?

e Do you want a cigarette?
v ¿Fumas?

f Are you hungry?
vi ¿Prefieres el vino tinto o el vino blanco?

g Would you like to go out to dinner?
vii ¿Te importa si fumo?

h Are you tired?
viii ¿Tienes una media naranja?

i Do you like sci-fi films?
ix ¿Tienes hambre?

j Have you got a man/woman in your life?
x ¿Te gustan las películas de ciencia-ficción?

Checklist: the *tú* form

You only use the **tú** form when speaking to younger children, pets and people you know very well, or people who have invited you to use it.

You do not use it to older people you do not know unless invited to do so.

The **tú** form sounds different from all others, so the actual word **tú** is not normally needed.

- The **tú** form of **-ar** verbs always ends in **-as** except for **estás**.
- The **tú** form of **-er** and **-ir** verbs always ends in **-es** except for **ir** – **vas. Ser** has an irregular stem – **eres**.
- Questions are formed by changing the intonation or by inverting the verb and the pronoun when there is one.

1.2.4 Talking about someone or something else: *él/ella* and *usted*

▶▶ **If you know how to use the él/ella/usted form, go on to the checklist on page 33.**

This form is called the third person. In English it is the *he/she/it* form of the verb. An important thing to remember is that this form is also used for **usted**, the formal word for *you*. As usual, the subject pronoun/person word is not normally used, because the verb endings are clear enough by themselves. However, **usted** is often used, especially in questions. Note that **usted** is often abbreviated to **Ud** or **Vd**.

> In Spanish, there is no word for *it*. Everything is masculine or feminine. **Una casa** (*a house*) is feminine, so you say *she* is old; **un libro** (*a book*) is masculine, so you say *he* is new.

The third person form is easy to learn, as it is the same as the **tú** form but without the **-s**, except for **ser** – **es** (*he/she/it is*).

(tú) vas	(él/ella/usted) va
(tú) tienes	(él/ella/usted) tiene
(tú) eres	(él/ella/usted) es

A *Él/ella/usted* and regular verbs

- The **él/ella/usted** form of **-ar** verbs ends in **-a** (like the **tú** form but without the final **-s**).
  (él/ella) compra; habla; lava

- The **él/ella/usted** form of **-er** verbs ends in **-e** (again, like the **tú** form but without the final **-s**).
  (él/ella) come; bebe; escoge

- The **él/ella/usted** form of **-ir** verbs also ends in **-e** (like the **tú** form but with no final **-s**).
  (él/ella) sube; vive; escribe

I Fill in the right part of the verb.

   a Usted ____ muchas cartas a los periódicos. (escribir)
   b Enrique Iglesias ____ canciones en español y en inglés. (cantar)
   c Mi hijo ____ por Internet. (navegar)
   d Su amiguita ____ muchas historias de Manolito Gafotas. (leer)
   e Doña Encarnación ____ muchos mensajes por e-mail. (recibir)
   f Don Ángel ____ su casa. (vender)
   g La señora Pérez ____ comprar una casa. (desear)
   h El banco ____ dinero a sus clientes. (prestar)
   i El abogado ____ los documentos del contrato de venta. (preparar)
   j La señora Pérez ____ el documento de venta delante del abogado. (firmar)

B *Él/ella/usted* and irregular verbs

Some of the most common, and most useful, verbs are, of course, irregular in this form – but remember, most of them are similar to the **tú** form but without the final **-s**.

infinitive	meaning	third person	meaning
estar	to be	está	he/she is/you are
ser	to be	es	he/she is/you are
ir	to go	va	he/she goes/you go

C *Él/ella/usted* and stem-changing verbs

The verbs which modify the spelling of their stem in the first and second persons do the same with **él/ella** and **usted**. Thus, the 'stretching' vowel **-e-** changes to **-ie-**, and **-o-** to **-ue-**. As before, a few have **-e-** to **-i-**, and just one has a change from **-u-** to **-ue-**.

stem change	infinitive	meaning	third person	meaning
e → ie	pensar querer preferir	to think to want to prefer	piensa quiere prefiere	he/she thinks/you think he/she wants/you want he/she prefers/you prefer
o → ue	contar volver dormir	to count to return to sleep	cuenta vuelve duerme	he/she counts/you count he/she returns/you return he/she sleeps/you sleep
e → i	pedir	to ask for	pide	he/she asks/you ask for
u → ue	jugar	to play	juega	he/she plays/you play

Note that **tener** is one of these verbs: the **él** form is **tiene**.

II   Choose a verb from the list above and complete each sentence with the correct form. Then, if you are feeling adventurous, translate them into English!

    a Mi amigo ____ al fútbol todos los domingos.
    b Su mujer ____ que esto es excesivo.
    c Le ____ un domingo sin fútbol.
    d Ella no ____ con él, porque es muy egoísta.
    e ____ ir a la playa con su marido.
    f Pero él ____ estar con sus amigos.
    g Después ____ a casa muy cansado.
    h Luego ____ hasta la hora de cenar.

III   How would you say the following?

    a El señor Pablos ____ madrileño. (ser)
    b ____ en Madrid. (vivir)
    c ____ a Algeciras. (ir)
    d ____ el tren. (coger)
    e ____ una noche en el tren. (pasar)
    f Al día siguiente, ____ a Algeciras. (llegar)
    g ____ dos grandes maletas. (tener)
    h ____ sus maletas en un carrito. (poner)
    i ____ a un taxi. (llamar)
    j Cuando se ____ , sus maletas ya no están. (volver)

D   *Él/ella/ usted* and reflexive verbs

The reflexive pronoun for the **él/ella** and **usted** form is **se**. In the following table, all the third person forms are also used for **usted**, the formal way of expressing *you*.

This form is often used to describe an action for which there is no known subject:

Se construye un nuevo hotel en Cádiz.   A new hotel is being built in Cádiz.

infinitive	meaning	third person	meaning
aburrirse	to get bored	se aburre	he/she gets/you get bored
acostarse	to go to bed	se acuesta	he/she goes/you go to bed
afeitarse	to shave	se afeita	he/she shaves/you shave
cansarse	to get tired	se cansa	he/she gets/you get tired
despertarse	to wake up	se despierta	he/she wakes up/you wake up
ducharse	to have a shower	se ducha	he/she has/you have a shower
lavarse	to wash (oneself)	se lava	he/she washes/you wash
levantarse	to get up	se levanta	he/she gets up/you get up
pasearse	to go for a walk	se pasea	he/she goes/you go for a walk
peinarse	to comb one's hair	se peina	he/she combs/you comb (hair)
secarse	to dry oneself	se seca	he/she dries/you dry (self)
sentarse	to sit down	se sienta	he/she sits/you sit down
vestirse	to get dressed	se viste	he/she gets/you get dressed

IV   What does Urbano do?

a ____ a las once. (despertarse)

b ____ a mediodía. (levantarse)

c ____ (afeitarse)

d ____ (ducharse)

e ____ los dientes. (lavarse)

f ____ con una toalla. (secarse)

g ____ (peinarse)

h ____ (vestirse)

i ____ a leer el periódico. (sentarse)

j ____ pronto. (aburrirse)

k ____ por el parque. (pasearse)

l ____ después de una hora. (cansarse)

m ____ temprano. (acostarse)

E   Saying that somebody else likes something

As we have seen, Spanish does not really have a verb for *to like*. Instead, it uses *to please* as a sort of 'back-to-front' way of conveying the idea of liking. The thing that changes is the personal pronoun which goes in front of the verb **gustar**: **¿le gusta esta casa?** – *does he/she like ...?* (literally: *does this house please him/her?*).

To talk about liking more than one thing, the verb adds **-n**:
le gustan estas casas – *he/she likes these houses* (literally: *these houses please him/her*).

Note that the verb agrees with the *thing liked*, which is the subject. The person liking is expressed by a pronoun. The same goes for the other similar expressions in 1.2.3, section E.

Remember also that this same form is used for **usted**, the formal word for *you*. So, to ask whether a stranger likes something:

¿Le gusta esta falda?   Do you like this skirt?
¿Le gustan estos guantes?   Do you like these gloves?

F   Using the *usted* form

V   Your employee is slacking. Tell him/her what he/she is doing.

a You read the paper in the   (Usted) _____ el periódico por la
morning.   mañana. (leer)

b You go to the toilet eight   _____ a los servicios ocho veces al
times a day.   día. (ir)

c You take two hours for your   Se _____ dos horas para el
lunch break.   almuerzo. (tomar)

d You sleep a good part of   _____ buena parte de la tarde.
the afternoon.   (dormir)

e You do the crossword in the   _____ el crucigrama por la tarde.
afternoon.   (hacer)

f You drink a scotch at   _____ un whisky a la hora del té.
tea break.   (tomar)

g You have to do something   _____ que hacer algo. (tener)
about it.

h What do you say in your   ¿Qué _____ usted en su defensa?
defence?   (decir)

Checklist: the *él/ella/usted* form

You use the **él/ella/usted** form when you are talking about someone or something, or when addressing somebody by the formal word for *you*, **usted**.

> The **él/ella/usted** form is like the **tú** form but without the final **-s**.

- The **él/ella/usted** form of regular **-ar** verbs is made by adding **-a** to the stem.
- The **él /ella/usted** form of regular **-er** verbs is made by adding **-e** to the stem.

- The **él/ella/usted** form of regular **-ir** verbs is made by adding **-e** to the stem.
- The most common irregular verbs are **estar** (**está**), **ser** (**es**) and **ir** (**va**).
- The reflexive pronoun for the **él/ella/usted** form is **se**: ¿**cómo se llama?**

1.2.5 Talking about yourself and someone else: nosotros/as

▶▶ **If you are not going to need to use this form, skip the rest of this section and go to the checklist on page 36, as you need to be able to recognise it when you hear it, even if you don't use it.**

You use the **nosotros/as** form (or the first person plural) where you use *we* in English, i.e. when talking about yourself and someone else: *we, my husband and I, my colleagues and I, my friend and I, Mrs Brown and I,* etc.

Note the two pronoun forms: **nosotros** for two or more men or a mixed group, and **nosotras** when *we* refers just to women. Remember that in Spanish the subject pronoun does not usually need to be expressed.

A Verbs that are regular in the nosotros/as form

The **nosotros/as** form is regular in almost all verbs. It is made by adding **-amos** to the stem of **-ar** verbs, **-emos** to **-er** verbs, and **-imos** to **-ir** verbs. (Remember: the stem is made by taking the **-ar/-er/-ir** off the infinitive. See 1.1.2.) This form is *not* affected by stem changes or spelling irregularities seen in the **yo, tú** and **él/ella/usted** forms.

Note that this form is often used with the idea of *Let's* ...

| ¡Vamos! | Let's go! |
| ¡Bailamos! | Let's dance! |

Some common verbs that are regular in the **nosotros/as** form; remember that each can be used for *we ...* or *we are ...ing*:

infinitive	meaning	first person plural	meaning
cambiar	to change	cambiamos	we change
coger	to take	cogemos	we take
comer	to eat	comemos	we eat
comprender	to understand	comprendemos	we understand
escoger	to choose	escogemos	we choose

infinitive	meaning	first person plural	meaning
hablar	to speak	hablamos	we speak
jugar	to play	jugamos	we play
quedar	to stay	quedamos	we stay
ver	to see	vemos	we see
terminar	to finish	terminamos	we finish
trabajar	to work	trabajamos	we work

B Verbs that are irregular in the *nosotros/as* form

All verbs end in **-mos**. The only common verbs with an irregular **nosotros/as** form are:

ser → somos – we are
ir → vamos – we go

I How would you say the following? Use the verbs given in brackets.

a We are working today. ____ hoy. (trabajar)
b We are playing volleyball tonight. ____ al voleibol esta tarde. (jugar)
c We are seeing friends at 6 p.m. ____ a unos amigos a las 18h00. (ver)
d We are dining in a restaurant. ____ en un restaurante. (cenar)
e We are going home at 10 p.m. ____ a las 22h00. (regresar)
f We are going to León tomorrow. ____ a León mañana. (ir)
g We are leaving at 8 a.m. ____ a las 8h00. (salir)
h We arrive at 11.15 a.m. ____ a las 11h15. (llegar)
i We buy our tickets at the station. ____ nuestros billetes en la estación. (comprar)
j We have lots of suitcases. ____ muchas maletas. (tener)

II How would you say the following in Spanish?

a We are English. Nosotros ____ ingleses.
b We speak Spanish. ____ español.
c We are going to Spain. ____ a España.
d We are choosing the day. ____ el día.
e We are taking the train. ____ el tren.
f We change trains in Paris. ____ de tren en París.
g We understand the instructions. ____ las instrucciones.
h We eat in a restaurant. ____ en un restaurante.
i We are working overtime this evening. ____ horas extras esta tarde.
j We finish at 6 p.m. ____ a las 18h00.
k We are playing tennis later. ____ al tenis más tarde.

C *Nosotros/as* with reflexive verbs

The reflexive form is made by adding **nos** in front of the verb. Note that the reflexive pronoun is **nos** for both masculine and feminine.

(Nosotros) nos llamamos Neil y John. We are called Neil and John.
(Nosotras) nos llamamos Jean y Ruth. We are called Jean and Ruth.

infinitive	meaning	first person plural	meaning
acostarse	to go to bed	nos acostamos	we go to bed
darse prisa	to hurry	nos damos prisa	we hurry
levantarse	to get up	nos levantamos	we get up
pasearse	to go for a walk	nos paseamos	we go for a walk
separarse	to get separated	nos separamos	we get separated

III How would you say the following?

a We wake up at seven o'clock.   _____ a las siete. (despertarse)
b We get up at eight o'clock.   _____ a las ocho. (levantarse)
c We go to bed at 11 p.m.   _____ a las 23h00. (acostarse)
d We are having a shower.   _____ (ducharse)
e We are hurrying.   _____ (darse prisa)
f We are getting dressed.   _____ (vestirse)
g We are getting washed.   _____ (lavarse)
h We go for a walk every morning.   _____ cada mañana. (pasearse)
i We are getting separated.   _____ (separarse)

D Saying that you and (an) other(s) like something

As we have seen, Spanish uses *to please* as a sort of 'back-to-front' way of conveying the idea of liking. To say that you and (an)other(s) like something, use **nos gusta esta playa** which literally means *this beach pleases us*.

To talk about liking more than one thing, the verb adds **-n**: **nos gustan estas naranjas** – *these oranges please us*.

For other similar 'back-to-front' expressions, see 1.2.2, section G.

Checklist: the *nosotros/as* form

- To talk about yourself and someone else (*we*), use **nosotros/as** in Spanish.
- All verbs end in **-mos**.
- Common irregular **nosotros/as** forms are: **ser** → **somos** and **ir** → **vamos**.
- The reflexive pronoun is **nos**.

a	we have	queremos
b	we are	leemos
c	we are staying	venimos
d	we are eating	no comprendemos
e	we can	podemos
f	we are not coming	somos
g	we do not understand	llegamos
h	we want	quedamos
i	we are going	tenemos
j	we are seeing	hacemos
k	we are leaving	no venimos
l	we are arriving	vamos
m	we are coming	comemos
n	we are doing	salimos
o	we are reading	vemos

Now cover up the Spanish and see if you can do them without help!

1.2.6 Talking to more than one person you know well: *vosotros/as*

▶▶ **If you know about the vosotros/as form, go on to the checklist on page 39.**

This is the plural equivalent of the **tú** form, and is the second person plural of the verb or 'familiar plural' form: it is used to talk to more than one person whom you would address as **tú**. Note the two pronoun forms: **vosotros** for two or more men or a mixed group, and **vosotras** when *you* refers just to women.

A Verbs that are regular in the *vosotros/as* form

The **vosotros/as** form is made by adding **-áis** to the stem of **-ar** verbs, **-éis** to **-er** verbs and **-ís** to **-ir** verbs. Only two common verbs are irregular in this form, so it is very easy to learn. As usual, the subject pronoun is normally unnecessary because the endings are so distinctive.

¿Habláis inglés?	Do you speak English?
¿Tenéis un coche español?	Have you got a Spanish car?
¿Vivís en España?	Do you live in Spain?

B Verbs that are irregular in the *vosotros/as* form

The two most common irregular **vosotros/as** forms are:

ser → sois – you are
ir → vais – you go

C *Vosotros/as* and asking questions

▶▶ **If you know all about asking questions, go straight on to 1.2.7.**

Questions are formed in the same way as in the **tú** and **usted** forms: by changing the intonation. Occasionally, for emphasis the pronoun is used, in which case it will usually come after the verb in a question.

¿Qué hacéis (vosotros) esta tarde?   What are you doing this evening?

I Cover up the Spanish and see if you can ask these questions.

a Are you going to the meeting? ¿Vais vosotros a la reunión?
b Have you got an appointment? ¿Tenéis una cita?
c Do you know the MD? ¿Conocéis al director?
d Can you operate the video link-up? ¿Sabéis usar el aparato de videoconferencia?
e Can you call your boss? ¿Podéis llamar a vuestro jefe?
f Do you have to go back to the hotel? ¿Tenéis que volver al hotel?
g Do you want to use the OHP? ¿Queréis usar el retroproyector?
h Can you (Do you) see the screen? ¿Veis la pantalla?
i Do you take notes? ¿Tomáis apuntes?
j Are you making a recording? ¿Estáis grabando vosotros?
k Are you ready? ¿Estáis listos?
l Do you understand? ¿Comprendéis?

D *Vosotros/as* and reflexive verbs

The reflexive pronoun for the **vosotros/as** form is **os** for both masculine and feminine.

¿Os las arregláis? Are you sorting yourselves out?
Os ocupáis del niño. You are looking after the child.
¿A qué hora os levantáis? What time do you get up?
¿A qué hora os acostáis? What time do you go to bed?

II Match the following English and Spanish phrases, then cover up the right-hand side and see if you can remember the Spanish.

a Can you remember this man? ¿Os vestís ya?
b Are you going for a walk in the park? ¿Os levantáis tarde?
c Are you getting dressed already? ¿Os despertáis temprano?
d Are you making fun of me? ¿Os acordáis de este hombre?
e Do you get up late ? ¿Os paseáis por el parque?
f Do you wake up early? ¿Os burláis de mí?

E   Asking whether more than one person likes something

As we have seen, Spanish uses 'to please' as a sort of 'back-to-front' way of conveying the idea of liking. To ask friends or relatives whether they like something, use **¿os gusta esta plaza?** which literally means *does this square please you?*

To talk about liking more than one thing, the verb adds **-n**: **¿os gustan estas peras?** – *do you like these pears?*

For other similar 'back-to-front' expressions, see 1.2.2 section G.

Checklist: the *vosotros/as* form

- The **vosotros/as** form is used when talking to more than one person whom you would address as **tú**.
- The **vosotros/as** form of regular verbs is made by adding **-áis**, **-éis** or **-ís** to the stem of the infinitive.

 Almost all verbs are regular.

- You are quite likely to use the **vosotros/as** form to ask questions:

¿Podéis decirme por dónde se va a ...?	Can you tell me the way to ...?
¿Sabéis ...?	Do you know (how to do something)?
¿Conocéis a la señora Jiménez?	Do you know Mrs Jiménez?
¿Dónde vivís?	Where do you live?

- Common irregular **vosotros/as** forms are: **-ser** → **sois** and **ir** → **vais**.

- The reflexive pronoun is **os**.

¡Os levantáis temprano!	You get up early!

- Questions are formed by intonation:

  ¿Tenéis coche?

1.2.7   Talking about other people and things: *ellos/ellas* and *ustedes*

This form is called the third person plural. In English it is the *they* form of the verb. An important thing to remember is that this form is also used for **ustedes**, the plural formal word for *you*. As usual, the subject pronoun/person word is not normally used, because the verb endings are clear enough by themselves. However, **ustedes** is often used, especially in questions. Note that **ustedes** is often abbreviated to **Uds** or **Vds**.

If you know all about the ellos/ellas/ustedes form, go on to the checklist on page 43.

A *Ellos/ellas/ustedes* and regular verbs
- The **ellos/ellas/ustedes** form of regular **-ar** verbs is made by adding **-an** to the stem.
- The **ellos/ellas/ustedes** form of regular **-er** verbs is made by adding **-en** to the stem.
- The **ellos/ellas/ustedes** form of regular **-ir** verbs is made by adding **-en** to the stem.

The **ellos/ellas/ustedes** form is the same as the **él/ella/usted** form, but with **-n** added. The subject pronoun is usually unnecessary, though it is often used in the case of **ustedes**, especially in questions. Where a pronoun is used for *they*, remember that **ellas** can only be used where only women are referred to, and **ellos** is used for all males or a mixed group.

(él) estudia – he is studying → (ellos) estudian – they are studying
(ella) charla – she is chatting → (ellas) charlan – they are chatting

(él) corre – he is running → (ellos) corren – they are running
(ella) come – she is eating → (ellas) comen – they are eating

(él) duerme – he is asleep → (ellos) duermen – they are asleep
(ella) sale – she is going out → (ellas) salen – they are going out

 Remember, you only use **ellas** if all the people (or things) referred to are feminine. If there is one male in the group, however many females there are, you have to use **ellos**.

B *Ellos/ellas/ustedes* and irregular verbs
These are in fact quite straightforward, because they too are like the **él/ella/usted** form but with **-n** added. The only verb with a completely irregular **ellos/ellas/ustedes** form is **ser**, as shown in the following table.

infinitive	meaning	3rd person singular	3rd person plural	meaning
estar	to be	está	están	they/you are
ser	to be	es	son	they/you are
ir	to go	va	van	they/you go

Ellos/ellas/ustedes and stem-changing verbs

The verbs which modify the spelling of their stem in the singular forms do the same with **ellos/ellas** and **ustedes**. Thus, the 'stretching' vowel **-e-** changes to **-ie-**, and **-o-** to **-ue-**. As before, a few have **-e-** to **-i-**, and just one has a change from **-u-** to **-ue-**.

Here are the most useful examples:

stem change	infinitive	meaning	3rd pers. plural	meaning
e → ie	p**e**nsar	to think	p**ie**nsan	they think/you think
	qu**e**rer	to want	qu**ie**ren	they want/you want
	pref**e**rir	to prefer	pref**ie**ren	they prefer/you prefer
o → ue	enc**o**ntrar	to find	enc**ue**ntran	they find/you find
	v**o**lver	to return	v**ue**lven	they return/you return
	d**o**rmir	to sleep	d**ue**rmen	they sleep/you sleep
e → i	p**e**dir	to ask for	p**i**den	they ask/you ask for
u → ue	j**u**gar	to play	j**ue**gan	they play/you play

Note that **tener** is one of these verbs: the **ellos/ellas/ustedes** form is **tienen**.

 Choose the verbs you think you may find useful and look for ways to remember them.

I Choose a verb from the list above and complete each sentence with the correct form. Then, if you are feeling adventurous, translate them into English!

a Mis amigos ____ al tenis todos los sábados.
b Sus mujeres ____ que es una pérdida de tiempo.
c Ellas ____ un poco de ayuda en casa.
d Ellas no ____ tiempo para divertirse.
e ____ ir de tiendas con sus maridos.
f Pero ellos ____ pasar el día con sus amigos.
g Después ____ a casa cansadísimos.
h Por eso ____ hasta la hora de cenar.

II What is happening? Fill in the correct form of the verbs.

a Los señores Pérez ____ ir de compras. (querer)
b ____ un coche nuevo. (tener)
c ____ al hipermercado. (ir)
d ____ el coche en el aparcamiento. (dejar)
e ____ sus compras. (hacer)

f ____ del hipermercado. (salir)
g Ya no ____ su coche. (encontrar)
h Lo ____ por todas partes. (buscar)
i No lo ____ . (ver)
j ____ a la policía. (llamar)

D *Ellos/ellas/ustedes* and reflexive verbs

The reflexive pronoun for the **ellos/ellas** and **ustedes** form is **se**. In the following table, all the third person forms are also used for **ustedes**, the formal way of expressing *you* in the plural.

> This form is often used to describe an action for which there is no known subject:
>
> Se construyen barcos en Cádiz.   Ships are built in Cádiz.

infinitive	meaning	third person plural	meaning
aburrirse	to get bored	se aburren	they/you get bored
acostarse	to go to bed	se acuestan	they/you go to bed
cansarse	to get tired	se cansan	they/you get tired
despertarse	to wake up	se despiertan	they/you wake up
ducharse	to have a shower	se duchan	they/you have a shower
irse	to go (away)	se van	they/you go (away)
lavarse	to wash (oneself)	se lavan	they/you wash
levantarse	to get up	se levantan	they/you get up
prepararse	to get ready	se preparan	they/you get ready
secarse	to dry oneself	se secan	they/you dry (self)
vestirse	to get dressed	se visten	they/you get dressed

III What do friends Francesca and Virginia do on their night out?

a ____ (despertarse)
b ____ (levantarse)
c ____ (ducharse)
d ____ (prepararse)
e ____ (salir)
f ____ a una bodega. (ir)
g Sus amigos no ____ (llegar)
h ____ (aburrirse)
i ____ (irse)

E   Saying that other people like something

As we have already seen, Spanish has no verb for *to like*, and instead uses *to please* as a 'back-to-front' way of expressing the idea of liking. The thing that changes is the personal pronoun which goes in front of the verb **gustar**: **¿Les gusta esta casa?** *Do they/you like this house?* (literally: *Does this house please them/you?*).

To talk about liking more than one thing, the verb adds **-n**: **Sí, les gustan estas casas**. *Yes, they/you like these houses.* (literally: *These houses please them/you.*)

The verb **gustar** agrees with the *thing liked*, which is the subject, and the person liking is expressed by a pronoun. The same goes for the other similar expressions in 1.2.2 section D. Remember also that this same form is used for **ustedes**, the formal word for *you* in the plural. So to ask whether other people like something, or to ask strangers whether they like something:

¿Les gusta este hotel?	Do they/you like this hotel?
¿Les gustan estas sillas?	Do they/you like these chairs?

F   Using the *ustedes* form

IV   You are a tourist guide. Explain to your group of tourists what they need to do.

a You get your room key from reception.
(Vds) _____ sus llaves en recepción. (obtener)

b You go to the dining room for dinner.
_____ al comedor para la cena. (ir)

c You can have a drink in the bar.
_____ tomar algo de beber en el bar. (poder)

d You need to get to bed early.
_____ acostarse temprano. (necesitar)

e You must get up at 7.
_____ que levantarse a las 7. (tener)

f You must have a good breakfast.
_____ desayunar bien. (deber)

g You will board the coach at 8 o'clock.
_____ al autocar a las 8. (subir)

h Tomorrow you travel to Málaga.
Mañana _____ a Málaga. (viajar)

Checklist: *ellos/ellas/ustedes* form

- You use the **ellos/ella/ustedes** form when you are talking about people or things, or when addressing somebody by the formal word for *you* in the plural, **ustedes**.

The **ellos/ellas/ustedes** form is like the **él/ella/usted** form with a final **-n**.

- The **ellos/ellas/ustedes** form of regular **-ar** verbs is made by adding **-an** to the stem.
- The **ellos/ellas/ustedes** form of regular **-er** verbs is made by adding **-en** to the stem.
- The **ellos/ellas/ustedes** form of regular **-ir** verbs is made by adding **-en** to the stem.
- The most common irregular verbs are **estar** (**están**), **ser** (**son**) and **ir** (**van**).
- The reflexive pronoun for the **ellos/ellas/ustedes** form is **se**: ¿cómo se llaman?

1.2.8 ▶Fast track: Present tense

Spanish verbs change their endings according to the person who is doing them. The endings all look and sound different, so in Spanish you don't usually need to use the personal pronoun.

There are a few irregular verbs and, unfortunately, some of them are useful everyday verbs, but you probably already know some of these.

Regular verbs

- **-ar** verbs
  Most Spanish verbs are **-ar** verbs.
  The regular endings for **-ar** verbs are **-o**; **-as**; **-a**; **-amos**; **-áis**; **-an**.
  All new verbs are **-ar** verbs, e.g. **faxear**, **chutar**.
  Most **-ar** verbs are regular, i.e. they follow the same pattern.

- **-er** verbs
  There are nowhere near as many **-er** verbs as there are **-ar** verbs.
  The regular endings for **-er** verbs are **-o**; **-es**; **-e**; **-emos**; **-éis**; **-en**.
  Most **-er** verbs are regular, i.e. they follow the same pattern.

Try to remember a phrase you might use, which includes a word you are trying to remember, e.g. **Siempre bebemos vino tinto**.

- **-ir** verbs
  There are not very many **-ir** verbs.
  The regular endings for **-ir** verbs are **-o**; **-es**; **-e**; **-imos**;
  -ís; **-en**.
  Most **-ir** verbs are regular, i.e. they follow the same
  pattern.
  Each ending sounds different, so the person word is not
  usually needed.

Irregular verbs

Here are some of the most useful irregular verbs:

ser – to be	**ir** – to go	**haber** – to have*
soy	voy	he
eres	vas	has
es	va	ha
somos	vamos	hemos
sois	vais	habéis
son	van	han

* only used to form the perfect and other compound tenses

These two verbs behave mostly like **-ar** verbs, but have a **yo**
form ending in **-oy**:

dar – to give	**estar** – to be	
d**oy**	est**oy**	(note the accents on the
das	estás	other persons of **estar**)
da	está	
damos	estamos	
dais	estáis	
dan	están	

These two also have an irregular **yo** form:

saber – to know	**ver** – to see
s**é**	v**eo**
sabes	ves
sabe	ve
sabemos	vemos
sabéis	veis
saben	ven

The following are some other verbs which have an irregularity just in the **yo** form. In each case the **-g-** serves to 'strengthen' the sound:

caer	hacer	oír	poner	salir	traer	valer
cai**g**o	ha**g**o	oi**g**o	pon**g**o	sal**g**o	trai**g**o	val**g**o
caes	haces	oyes*	pones	sales	traes	vales
cae	hace	oye*	pone	sale	trae	vale
caemos	hacemos	oímos	ponemos	salimos	traemos	valemos
caéis	hacéis	oís	ponéis	salís	traéis	valéis
caen	hacen	oyen*	ponen	salen	traen	valen

* note the change from **i → y** in some forms of **oír**

 All verbs based on these perform in the same way, e.g. **componer**, **deshacer**.

Several verbs have a different way of strengthening the **yo** form, or of changing its spelling to keep the same consonant sound:

conocer	conducir	coger
cono**z**co	condu**z**co	co**j**o
conoces	conduces	coges
conoce	conduce	coge
conocemos	conducimos	cogemos
conocéis	conducís	cogéis
conocen	conducen	cogen

 Verbs based on these, such as **reconocer**, **reducir** and **recoger**, behave in the same way.

Stem-changing verbs

The following are examples of verbs which have a stem spelling change in person forms where the stress falls on the stem:

e → ie			o → ue			e → i	u → ue
p**e**nsar	qu**e**rer	pref**e**rir	c**o**ntar	v**o**lver	d**o**rmir	p**e**dir	j**u**gar
p**ie**nso	qu**ie**ro	pref**ie**ro	c**ue**nto	v**ue**lvo	d**ue**rmo	p**i**do	j**ue**go
p**ie**nsas	qu**ie**res	pref**ie**res	c**ue**ntas	v**ue**lves	d**ue**rmes	p**i**des	j**ue**gas
p**ie**nsa	qu**ie**re	pref**ie**re	c**ue**nta	v**ue**lve	d**ue**rme	p**i**de	j**ue**ga
pensamos	queremos	preferimos	contamos	volvemos	dormimos	pedimos	jugamos
pensáis	queréis	preferís	contáis	volvéis	dormís	pedís	jugáis
p**ie**nsan	qu**ie**ren	pref**ie**ren	c**ue**ntan	v**ue**lven	d**ue**rmen	p**i**den	j**ue**gan

Notice how the stem spelling only changes in person forms 1, 2, 3 and 6, the forms in which the stress is on the 'stretchy vowel'; you could call them '1-2-3-6 verbs' to remind you which forms have this change. If you arrange them like this ...

... you could even call them 'boot verbs'! The forms inside the boot-shape change, those outside do not. In fact, the **nosotros/as** and **vosotros/as** forms of almost all verbs are regular, i.e. they are close to the infinitive form.

These verbs have an irregular **yo** form as well as stem spelling changes:

e → ie		e → i
tener	venir	decir
tengo	vengo	digo
tienes	vienes	dices
tiene	viene	dice
tenemos	venimos	decimos
tenéis	venís	decís
tienen	vienen	dicen

I You are talking about yourself. Use the verbs in brackets.

a (Yo) ____ una reunión con uno de mis colegas. (tener)
b ____ listo/a. (estar)
c ____ al centro. (ir)
d ____ el metro. (coger)
e ____ en la estación de Plaza de Toros. (bajar)
f ____ del metro. (salir)
g ____ la plaza. (cruzar)
h ____ a mi colega delante de la Plaza de Toros. (esperar)
i No ____ esperar mucho. (querer)
j Después de media hora ____ al hotel. (volver)

II   Still using the same sentences, ask someone you know really well the same things. Use the **tú** form. For example:

¿*Tienes* (tú) una reunión con uno de tus colegas?

a ¿____ (tú) una reunión con uno de tus colegas? (tener)
b ¿____ listo/a? (estar)
c ¿____ al centro? (ir)
d ¿____ el metro? (coger)
e ¿____ en la estación de Plaza de Toros? (bajar)
f ¿____ del metro? (salir)
g ¿____ la plaza? (cruzar)
h ¿____ a tu colega delante de la Plaza de Toros? (esperar)
i ¿No ____ esperar mucho? (querer)
j Después de media hora ¿____ al hotel? (volver)

III   Now report back in the singular, saying he/she does it. Choose the correct verb from the three in brackets. For example:

(Él/Ella) *tiene* una reunión con uno de sus colegas.

a (Él/Ella) ____ una reunión con uno de sus colegas. (tiene está sale)
b ____ listo/a. (pone está sube)
c ____ al centro. (va es vale)
d ____ el metro. (coge reconoce compra)
e ____ en la estación de Plaza de Toros. (llega baja da)
f ____ del metro. (sale sube sabe)
g ____ la plaza. (trabaja corre cruza)
h ____ a su colega delante de la Plaza de Toros. (escucha mira espera)
i No ____ esperar mucho. (puede quiere vuelve)
j Después de media hora ____ al hotel. (vuelve hace coge)

IV   Now you are talking about yourself and a partner: say we do (or don't do) the same things. For example:

(Nosotros/as) *tenemos* una reunión con uno de nuestros colegas.

a (Nosotros/as) ____ una reunión con uno de nuestros colegas.
b ____ listos/as.
c ____ al centro.
d ____ el metro.
e ____ en la estación de Plaza de Toros.
f ____ del metro.
g ____ la plaza.
h ____ a nuestro colega delante de la Plaza de Toros.
i No ____ esperar mucho.
j Después de media hora ____ al hotel.

V   Using the same sentences, ask some other friends the same things. Use the **vosotros/as** form. For example:

¿*Tenéis* (vosotros/as) una reunión con uno de vuestros colegas?

a ¿____ (vosotros/as) una reunión con uno de vuestros colegas? (tener)
b ¿____ listos/as? (estar)
c ¿____ al centro? (ir)
d ¿____ el metro? (coger)
e ¿____ en la estación de Plaza de Toros? (bajar)
f ¿____ del metro? (salir)
g ¿____ la plaza? (cruzar)
h ¿____ a vuestro colega delante de la Plaza de Toros? (esperar)
i ¿No ____ esperar mucho? (querer)
j Después de media hora ¿____ al hotel? (volver)

VI Finally, say that they do it. Choose the correct verb. For example:

(Ellos/Ellas) *tienen* una reunión con uno de sus colegas.

a (Ellos/Ellas) ____ una reunión con uno de sus colegas. (tienen bajan salen)
b ____ listos/as. (están son suben)
c ____ al centro. (van ponen valen)
d ____ el metro. (cogen reconocen saben)
e ____ en la estación de Plaza de Toros. (llegan están bajan)
f ____ del metro. (salen suben compran)
g ____ la plaza. (escuchan miran cruzan)
h ____ a su colega delante de la Plaza de Toros. (trabajan corren esperan)
i No ____ esperar mucho. (pueden quieren cogen)
j Después de media hora ____ al hotel. (vuelven pueden cogen)

1.3 Negatives, interrogatives and imperatives

▶▶ **If you know what these are, go on to 1.3.1.**

- The **negative** is used to say *no* you *don't* do something, you *haven't* got something or to tell someone *not* to do something. A negative sentence is a sentence with a *no, not* or *don't* in it.
- The **interrogative** is used to ask questions.
- The **imperative** is used to give orders, directions or instructions: to tell someone what to do or what not to do!

1.3.1 Negatives: how to say what you don't do

▶▶ **If you know how to use no ..., go on to 1.3.2.**

To say you don't do something, you put **no** in front of the verb.

No sé.   I don't know.

No means *not*, as above, and also *No*, ... so you often see and hear it twice at the beginning of a sentence:

No, no sé.   No, I don't know.

I   Say you/they don't do these things by putting **no** in front of the verb. Say the sentences aloud to get used to the sound.

a They don't drink wine.   _____ vino. (beber)
b I don't often write letters.   _____ cartas a menudo. (escribir)
c She doesn't read her e-mails.   _____ su correo electrónico. (leer)
d We don't buy magazines.   _____ revistas. (comprar)
e I don't know!   ¡_____ !(saber)
f He can't find the entrance.   _____ encontrar la entrada. (poder)
g They are not coming tonight.   _____ esta tarde. (venir)
h I don't want to go.   _____ ir. (querer)
i We don't like going there.   _____ ir allí. (gustar – be careful with this one!)
j You don't eat garlic!   ¡_____ el ajo! (comer – tú)

1.3.2   Interrogatives: asking questions

There are four ways of asking a question. You can:

- make a statement and change the intonation;
- invert the subject and the verb where a subject pronoun is used;
- use a question word, and then the verb as normal;
- use a question word and invert the subject and verb where a subject pronoun is used.

In the following sections, read the examples and then cover up the English and see if you understand the meanings; then cover up the Spanish and see if you can put the questions back into Spanish. Note that questions *always* start with an inverted question mark in written Spanish.

A   Changing the intonation

This is the easiest and most used way to ask a question. Remember, you have to use a rising tone towards the end of the question, which is what identifies a question when spoken. In written form, the inverted question mark at the start of the sentence shows that a question is on the way. Practise saying them aloud.

¿Entiendes?	You understand?
¿Habla inglés?	Do you speak English?
¿Conocéis el Hotel Soberano?	You know the Hotel Soberano?
¿Miguel sabe latín?	Does Miguel know Latin?
¿Este tren va a Ciudad Rodrigo?	Is this train going to Ciudad Rodrigo?

B Inverting the subject and the verb

This can be done where the subject pronoun is used for extra emphasis, being most common with **usted** and **ustedes**. It can also be done where a name or noun is used as the subject.

¿Entiendes tú?	Do you understand?
¿Habla usted inglés?	Do you speak English?
¿Conocéis vosotros el Hotel Soberano?	Do you know the Hotel Soberano?
¿Sabe Miguel latín?	Does Miguel know Latin?
¿Va este tren a Cádiz?	Is this train going to Cádiz?

C Using a question word followed by the verb as normal

¿Qué dices?	What are you saying?
¿Por qué hace esto?	Why are you doing this?
¿Dónde os alojáis?	Where are you staying?
¿Cómo van a Palencia?	How are they going to Palencia?
¿A quién conoce?	Whom do you know?
¿Cuántos euros tenéis?	How many euros do you have?
El tren, ¿cuándo llega a Cádiz?	When does the train arrive at Cádiz?

Notice where the inverted question mark goes in the last example.

D Using a question word and inverting the subject and verb

¿Qué dices tú?	What are you saying?
¿Por qué hace usted esto?	Why are you doing this?
¿Dónde os alojáis vosotros?	Where are you staying?
¿Cómo van ellos a Palencia?	How are they going to Palencia?
¿A quién conoce usted?	Whom do you know?
¿Cuántos euros tenéis vosotros?	How many euros do you have?
¿Cuándo llega el tren a Cádiz?	When does the train arrive at Cádiz?

Note that *all* question words have an accent.

I   Use method B to turn these statements into questions. For example:

¿Viven los señores Blanco en Madrid?

a Los señores Blanco viven en Madrid.
b Salen de vacaciones.
c Cogen el tren.
d Van a la Costa del Sol.
e Tienen un apartamento allí.
f Alquilan un coche.
g Juegan al golf.
h Hacen esquí acuático.
i Tienen unos amigos en Fuengirola.
j Por la tarde cenan en un restaurante.

II   Use method D with these question words. For example:

¿Adónde van ellos?

a Where are they going?	¿Adónde _____? (ir)
b When are they leaving?	¿Cuándo _____? (salir)
c How are they travelling?	¿Cómo _____ ? (viajar)
d Why are they in Barcelona?	¿Por qué _____ en Barcelona? (estar)
e What are they doing?	¿Qué _____ ? (hacer)
f Who are they meeting?	¿Con quién _____ una reunión? (tener)
g How long are they staying at the hotel?	¿Cuánto tiempo se _____ en el hotel? (quedar)

1.3.3   Imperatives: giving orders, directions or instructions

▶▶   **If you know about the imperative, go on to 1.3.4.**

The imperative is the part of the verb you use when you are telling someone to do something, or giving instructions or an order: *Watch out! Stop! Turn left!* etc.

In Spanish, since there are four ways of saying *you*, there are four ways of telling somebody what to do!

You use the **tú** form only when speaking to someone you know well or someone younger than you, and the **vosotros/as** form for two or more people you know well.

You use the **usted** form for a stranger or somebody senior to you, and the **ustedes** form for two or more strangers.

Look at these examples. Some are for **tú** and some for **usted**. You will probably have heard some of these before. Which ones do you know already?

Come on!	¡Venga!
Go!	¡Anda!
Cross the road!	¡Cruce la calle!
Turn left!	¡Gire a la izquierda!
Listen!	¡Escucha!
Wait!	¡Espere!
Hold the line! (telephone)	¡No cuelgue!
Hurry up!	¡Date prisa!

A Giving advice or instructions in the *tú* form

The **tú** imperative is used to give advice, instructions and orders to a single family member or friend. This is easy to form: simply take the **-s** off the normal **tú** form of the verb.

Buy a new tie!	¡Compra una corbata nueva!
Drink Rioja wine!	¡Bebe vino de Rioja!
Get in carefully!	¡Sube con cuidado!

The following table gives examples of regular, stem-changing and irregular imperatives in the **tú** form, as well as a reflexive verb.

infinitive	meaning	tú imperative	meaning
hablar	to speak	¡habla!	speak!
vender	to sell	¡vende!	sell!
escribir	to write	¡escribe!	write!
contar	to count	¡cuenta!	count!
volver	to return	¡vuelve!	return!
pedir	to ask for	¡pide!	ask for!
decir	to say	¡di!	say!
hacer	to do/make	¡haz!	do!/make!
ir	to go	¡ve!	go!
ser	to be	¡sé!	be!
poner	to put	¡pon!	put!
tener	to have	¡ten!	have!
venir	to come	¡ven!	come!
salir	to leave/go out	¡sal!	leave!/go out!
callarse	to shut up	¡cállate!	shut up!

Notice how, in the case of reflexive verbs, the reflexive pronoun is tacked onto the end of the imperative verb form and an accent is placed strategically to keep the stress in the right place.

A special form of the verb is used for giving negative commands in the **tú** form. This is easy to form: add **-es** to the stem of **-ar** verbs, and **-as** to the stem of **-er** and **-ir** verbs.

¡No te preocupes!   Don't worry!
¡No comas eso!   Don't eat that!
¡No subas la escalera!   Don't go up the stairs!

Note how the reflexive pronoun goes in front of the negative imperative.

For irregular stems for these negative commands, see section C.

I   Tell a friend or relative to do or not to do these things.

   a   Shut up!   ¡____! (callarse) (add reflexive pronoun to end: accent needed?)

   b   Don't sit down!   ¡No ____! (sentarse)
   c   Be careful!   ¡____ cuidado! (tener)
   d   Give me that!   ¡____ me eso! (dar)
   e   Be good!   ¡____ bueno/a! (ser)
   f   Don't come here!   ¡____ aquí! (venir)
   g   Get out of here!   ¡____ de aquí! (salir)
   h   Get up!   ¡____! (levantarse

B   Giving advice or instructions in the *vosotros/as* form

For giving orders and instructions to more than one relative or friend, use the *vosotros* imperative. This is based on the infinitive, replacing final **-r** with **-d** (for a change, there are no irregulars!):

¡Esperad!   Wait!   ¡Escuchad!   Listen!

A special form of the verb is used for giving negative commands. This is easy to form: add **-éis** to the stem of **-ar** verbs, and **-áis** to the stem of **-er** and **-ir** verbs.

¡No os preocupéis!   Don't worry!
¡No bebáis eso!   Don't drink that!
¡No subáis la escalera!   Don't go up the stairs!

For irregular stems for these negative commands, see section C.

C   Giving advice or instructions in the *usted* form

The **usted** form of address is the one most likely to be used to give advice, instructions and orders to a stranger or in public places. A special form of the verb is used for this: the subjunctive. This is easy to form: add **-e** to the stem of **-ar** verbs, and **-a** to the stem of **-er** and **-ir** verbs. The same verb form is used for negative commands:

¡No compre este coche!   Don't buy this car!
¡Beba LocaCola!   Drink LocaCola!
¡Suba con cuidado!   Get in carefully!

Some irregular verbs have a special stem based on the irregular **yo** form, and others have the stem change seen in the present tense. Note that, in the case of reflexive verbs, the reflexive pronoun is added to the end of the imperative verb form and an accent is added to keep the stress in the right place.

to sit down – sentarse → ¡siéntese! – sit down!

Here are some examples of regular, stem-changing, irregular and reflexive imperatives in the **usted** form:

infinitive	meaning	usted imperative form	meaning
hablar	to speak	¡hable!	speak!
comer	to eat	¡coma!	eat!
escribir	to write	¡escriba!	write!
contar	to count	¡cuente!	count!
volver	to return	¡vuelva!	return!
dormir	to sleep	¡duerma!	sleep!
decir	to say/tell	¡diga!	tell me!
hacer	to do	¡haga!	do!
introducir	to put in/ enter/introduce	¡introduzca!	put in!/ enter!/introduce!
ir	to go	¡vaya!	go!
oír	to hear/listen	¡oiga!	listen!
venir	to come	¡venga!	come!
acostarse	to go to bed	¡acuéstese!	go to bed!

II   What do these mean? Match them up.

a Enter your PIN.
b Pull.
c Wait for the tone.
d Speak into the microphone.
e Sign here.

f Cancel your (bus/train) ticket.
g Press.
h Please hold the line (don't hang up).
i Wait.
j Press the button.
k Listen, please. (when making a call)

i   Firme aquí.
ii   Pulse.
iii   Espere.
iv   Introduzca su número secreto.
v   Cancele su billete (de autobús/tren).
vi   Por favor, no cuelgue.
vii Oiga, por favor.
viii Diga/Dígame.

ix   Pulse el botón.
x   Tire.
xi   Espere el tono.

l Hello. (tell me – when answering phone) (also used for *excuse me/can you tell me*)

xii Hable cerca del micrófono.

III Tick the expressions in exercise II that you know already. Highlight any which are different from what you would have expected and choose three new ones to try to remember.

IV Your assistant is not well. Give him/her some advice.

a You look ill.   ____ enfermo/a. (parecer – not an imperative for this one)

b Go to see the doctor.   ____ a ver al médico. (ir)

c Drink more water.   ____ más agua. (beber)

d Eat more fruit.   ____ más fruta. (comer)

e Walk to work more.   ____ andando al trabajo. (venir)

f Smoke less.   ____ menos. (fumar)

g Go jogging.   ____ footing. (hacer)

h Get some fresh air.   ____ un poco de aire fresco. (tomar)

i Go to bed earlier.   ____ más temprano. (acostarse)

j Sleep well.   ____ bien. (dormir)

D   Giving advice or instructions in the *ustedes* form

The **ustedes** form of address is the one most likely to be used to give advice, instructions and orders to strangers or in public places. A special form of the verb is used for this: the subjunctive. This is easy to form: add **-en** to the stem of **-ar** verbs, and **-an** to the stem of **-er** and **-ir** verbs.

Buy your SEAT Ibiza now!	¡Compren su SEAT Ibiza ahora!
Drink CocaLoca!	¡Beban CocaLoca!
Suffer in silence!	¡Sufran en silencio!

Some irregular verbs have a special stem based on the irregular **yo** form, and others have the stem change seen in the present tense.

Note that, in the case of reflexive verbs, the reflexive pronoun is added to the end of the imperative, and an accent is added to keep the stress in the right place.

to sit down – sentarse → ¡siéntense! – sit down!

This same form of the verb is used for giving negative commands:

¡No se sienten!	Don't sit down!
¡No coman en este restaurante!	Don't eat at this restaurant!
¡No escriban en el muro!	Don't write on the wall!

Here are some examples of regular, irregular, stem-changing and reflexive imperatives in the **ustedes** form:

infinitive	meaning	ustedes imperative form	meaning
hablar	to speak	____	speak!
comer	to eat	____	eat!
escribir	to write	____	write!
contar	to count	¡cuenten!	count!
volver	to return	¡vuelvan!	return!
dormir	to sleep	¡duerman!	____
decir	to say/tell	¡digan!	tell me!
hacer	to do	¡hagan!	do!
introducir	to put in/enter/ introduce	¡introduzcan!	put in!/enter!/ introduce!
ir	to go	¡vayan!	____
oír	to hear/listen	¡oigan!	listen!
venir	to come	¡vengan!	____
acostarse	to go to bed	¡acuéstense!	____

V Fill in the gaps in the table above! Highlight any forms which are different from what you would have expected and choose three new ones to try to remember.

VI How would you give these instructions? If you are likely to need to use the **tú** form (**¡Come las verduras! ¡Ve a la cama!**) practise this form; otherwise concentrate on the **usted** form. Both sets of answers are given.

a ¡____ a la izquierda! (girar)
b ¡____ la escalera! (subir)
c ¡____ la primera calle a la derecha! (coger)
d ¡____ todo recto! (seguir)
e ¡____ hasta el próximo semáforo! (ir)
f ¡____ a la derecha y a la izquierda! (mirar)
g ¡____ la calle! (cruzar)
h ¡____ el autobús! (coger)
i ¡____ delante del teatro! (bajar)
j ¡____ me un mensaje corto (sms) cuando llegues/llegue! (mandar)

VII These instructions are from a recipe for Spanish omelette. Put them in the **tú** form.

a Preheat the oven. — ____ el horno. (precalentar)
b Chop the potatoes. — ____ las patatas. (picar)
c Beat the eggs. — ____ los huevos. (batir)
d Put the potatoes into a bowl. — ____ las patatas en una fuente. (meter)
e Add the oil and the beaten eggs. — ____ el aceite y los huevos batidos. (añadir)
f Mix well. — ____ bien. (mezclar)

g Warm up a frying pan.   ____ una sartén. (calentar)
h Pour the mixture into the   ____ la mezcla en la sartén.
    pan.   (verter)
i Fry the omelette slowly.   ____ a fuego lento. (freír)

VIII How would you tell someone to do these things? Use the **usted** form.

a Spend less time watching   ____ menos tiempo viendo la tele.
    television.   (pasar)
b Eat more vegetables.   ____ más verduras. (comer)
c Drink more water.   ____ más agua. (beber)
d Go jogging.   ____ footing. (hacer)
e Close the door.   ____ la puerta. (cerrar)
f Open the window.   ____ la ventana. (abrir)
g Show your passport.   ____ su pasaporte. (presentar)
h Speak more slowly.   ____ más despacio. (hablar)
i Come with me.   ____ conmigo. (venir)

IX Let's try a keep fit session. Give the **vosotros** form of the verbs in brackets, taking particular care with reflexives.

a Come in!   ¡____! (entrar)
b Get in line.   ____ una fila. (formar)
c Find a space.   ____ un espacio. (buscar)
d Run to the wall.   ____ hasta la pared. (correr)
e Stand with your feet apart.   ____ con los pies separados.
                                     (quedarse)
f Stretch your arms.   ____ los brazos. (estirar)
g Do five press-ups.   ____ cinco flexiones. (hacer)
h Lower your shoulders.   ____ los hombros. (bajar)
i Bend your knees.   ____ las rodillas. (doblar)
j Relax!   ____ (descansar)

X Tell some Spanish visitors the way to the town hall, using the **ustedes** form.

a Primero, ____ de aquí. (salir)
b ____ a la derecha. (girar)
c ____ la segunda calle a la derecha. (coger)
d ____ todo derecho. (continuar)
e ____ la plaza. (cruzar)
f ____ la calle hasta la rotonda. (seguir)
g ____ a la derecha: el ayuntamiento está enfrente. (torcer)

E   Telling someone what not to do

As you have seen, you introduce a negative imperative with the word **no**. However, whilst the four *you* forms have different ways of forming the imperative, in the negative they all use the appropriate subjunctive forms (see 1.6).

This special part of the verb is formed by adding a set of endings based on **-e** to the stem of **-ar** verbs, and a set of endings based on **-a** to the stem of **-er** and **-ir** verbs.

Note that the reflexive pronoun and other object pronouns go in front of negative imperatives.

XI First match the English and Spanish, then cover up the right-hand side of the page and see if you can remember the Spanish.

a Don't open the door. (tú)	i No beba el agua.
b Don't walk on the grass. (ustedes)	ii No ponga sus botas en el mostrador.
c Don't eat in the shop. (vosotros)	iii No esperéis aquí.
d Don't drink the water. (usted)	iv No dejes tu equipaje aquí.
e Don't cross the road here. (vosotros)	v No comáis en la tienda.
f Don't lean out of the window. (ustedes)	vi No fumen.
g Don't leave your luggage here. (tú)	vii No pisen la hierba.
h Don't wait here. (vosotros)	viii No crucéis la calle aquí.
i Don't put your boots on the counter. (usted)	ix No abras la puerta.
j Don't wear black. (tú)	x No se asomen por la ventanilla.
k Don't smoke. (ustedes)	xi No te vistas de negro.

1.3.4 ▶Fast track: Negatives, interrogatives and imperatives

A Negatives: saying you don't do something
You put **no** in front of the verb.

No sé.	I don't know.
No vende su coche.	He isn't selling his car.
No puedo venir.	I can't come.

B Interrogatives: asking questions
You can:

- make a statement and change the intonation: **¿Vas a Madrid?**
- invert the subject and the verb when a subject pronoun or the name or word for the subject is expressed: **¿Va usted a Madrid?**
- use a question word, then the verb as normal: **¿Adónde vas?**

- use a question word, then invert the expressed subject and verb: **¿Adónde va María?**

Useful question words (note they all have an accent):

¿Cuánto/a/os/as?	How much?
¿Cómo?	How? Pardon?
¿Dónde?	Where?
¿Por qué?	Why?
¿Cuándo?	When?
¿Qué?	What?
¿Quién?	Who?

C Imperatives: giving orders, directions and instructions

To make the imperative when talking to a child, family member or friend, you use a form usually based on the **tú** form of the present tense without the final **-s**.

¡Espera!   Wait!

There are some irregular forms:

¡Ve!   Go!
¡Ven de prisa!   Come quickly!

For **vosotros/as** imperatives, when speaking to two or more children, family members or friends, use a form based on the infinitive, replacing the final **-r** with **-d**:

¡Esperad!
¡Id!
¡Venid de prisa!

To make the **usted** imperative, when talking to a stranger or senior, you use a subjunctive form usually based on the **yo** form of the present tense without the final **-o**, adding **-e** for **-ar** verbs and **-a** for **-er** and **-ir** verbs.

¡Espere!

There are some irregular forms:

¡Vaya!
¡Venga de prisa!

For the **ustedes** imperative, when talking to two or more strangers or seniors, you use the **usted** imperative and add **-n**.

¡Esperen!

There are some irregular forms:

¡Vayan!
¡Vengan de prisa!

The appropriate form of the subjunctive is used for all negative imperatives.

1.4 The past tenses

You use the past tenses to say what you have done or what has happened.

▶▶ **If you know when to use the perfect, imperfect and preterite tenses, go on to 1.4.1.**

In Spanish, just as in English, there are different ways of expressing the past. The tenses you will need to use most are the perfect, the imperfect and the preterite tenses.

A The perfect tense (*el perfecto*)

The perfect tense is so called because it describes a single, completed action. Like the English equivalent, it is mostly used for an action in the immediate past, one which has just happened. It is probably the easiest Spanish tense, and is much more straightforward than its French equivalent.

I have eaten	he comido
I have arrived	he llegado

The perfect tense translates *I have played* and *I played*, and the question forms *Have you played?* and *Did you play?*

You use the perfect tense when you are talking or asking about something which happened and finished in the very recent past.

Ask yourself: Did it happen once in the recent past? Is it over? Is it finished? Then use the **perfect** tense.

B The imperfect tense (*el imperfecto*)

The imperfect tense translates *I was playing when ...*, *Were you playing when ...?* and *I used to play (a long time ago)*, and is used for repeated actions and descriptions in the past.

You use the imperfect tense:

- to talk about what used to happen in general:
  I used to go to school by bus. Iba a la escuela en el autobús.

- to describe things in the past:
  It was always raining. Llovía todo el tiempo.

* to say what was happening when something else happened (an interrupted action):

I was having a shower when he arrived.

Me duchaba cuando llegó.

Note how in the last example the single completed action is described in the preterite.

 Ask yourself: Did it use to happen in the past? Was it happening when something else happened? If you can use *was/were* + another verb in English, you use the **imperfect** in Spanish.

C   The preterite tense (*el pretérito*)

The preterite tense is so called because it describes a single, completed action at a specific moment in the (not recent) past; like the English equivalent – the past simple – it is mostly used for an action in the distant past, but it is sometimes used for an action which has just happened, as in American usage of English. It is not the easiest Spanish tense to form, but at least it is easy to decide when to use it: where we use the past simple in English.

I dined out yesterday evening.   Anoche cené fuera.
I arrived before the train.   Llegué antes que el tren.

The preterite translates *I played*, and the question form *Did you play?*

You use the preterite tense when you are talking or asking about something which happened and finished in the (usually not very recent) past.

 Ask yourself: Did it happen once in the past? Is it over? Is it finished? Then use the **preterite** tense or, if very recent, use the **perfect** tense.

I   Which tense are you going to use?

a Yesterday I went to town.
b I bought a new pair of trainers.
c Then I went to the gym.
d I used to go three times a week.
e I met my girlfriend at the gym.

f She was on the rowing machine.
g I was doing weights.
h She was laughing at me.
i I asked her why.
j My shorts were inside out.

1.4.1 The perfect tense

▶▶ **If you know how to form the perfect tense with haber, go on to 1.4.2.**

The perfect tense in Spanish is made up of two parts like the English perfect tense: part of the 'auxiliary' or 'helper' verb **haber** (*to have*) and the past participle.

Note that **haber** is only used for compound tenses such as the perfect, whilst **tener** is used for *to have* in the sense of possession.

to have	past participle	haber	participio pasado
I have	spoken	he	hablado
he has	eaten	ha	comido
we have	lived	hemos	vivido

In Spanish, all verbs form the perfect with **haber**. To get used to the sound of the perfect tense, choose one of the phrases below, or make up one of your own, and practise saying it until you are really fluent. Note that all of the following examples would be more likely to be expressed using the preterite tense.

He ido al bar y he pedido una cerveza.	I went to the bar and I ordered a beer.
Has perdido un cuchillo y has roto una taza.	You have lost a knife and broken a cup.
Ha ido al pueblo y ha hecho las compras.	He/She went to town and did some shopping.
Hemos ido a la estación y hemos cogido el tren de las seis.	We went to the station and we got the 6 o'clock train.
Habéis olvidado las llaves y habéis abandonado el coche.	You have forgotten the keys and abandoned the car.
Han ido al mercado y han comprado peras.	They went to the market and bought pears.

Here is the full present tense of the verb **haber**:

haber – to have
he
has
ha
hemos
habéis
han

I Practise with the following. How would you say ...?

a I have spoken   _____ hablado
b you have spoken (tú)   _____ hablado
c she has spoken   _____ hablado
d they have spoken   _____ hablado
e you have eaten (ustedes)   _____ comido
f we have eaten   _____ comido
g have you eaten? (vosotros)   ¿_____ comido?
h John has lived   _____ vivido
i you have lived (usted)   _____ vivido
j my wife and I have lived   _____ vivido

II Who watched the Telediario news bulletin? Complete these sentences by adding the correct form of **haber**.

a (Nosotros) _____ visto el Telediario de las 10h.
b (Ellos) _____ visto el Telediario de las 10h.
c (Usted) _____ visto el Telediario de las 10h.
d (Pili) _____ visto el Telediario de las 10h.
e (Vosotros) _____ visto el Telediario de las 10h.
f (Ustedes) _____ visto el Telediario de las 10h.
g (Tú) _____ visto el Telediario de las 10h.
h (Yo) _____ visto el Telediario de las 10h.
i (Paco) _____ visto el Telediario de las 10h.
j (Ella) _____ visto el Telediario de las 10h.

Checklist: the perfect tense

To make the perfect tense you use the right person of **haber** (*to have*) + the past participle.

haber: he, has, ha, hemos, habéis, han

1.4.2 How to form the past participle

▶▶ **If you know how to form the past participle, go on to 1.4.3.**

A Regular verbs

In English, the past participle of regular verbs is formed by adding *-ed* to the infinitive:

play → played; watch → watched; dance → danced

In Spanish, **-ar**, **-er** and **-ir** verbs form their past participles in different ways. You take off the ending (**-ar**, **-er** or **-ir**) and add the following:

hablar → hablado; comer → comido; vivir → vivido

-ar verbs	-er and -ir verbs
-ado	-ido

I Using these rules, what would the past participles of these verbs be?

a jugar		**k** lavar	
b comer		**l** pedir	
c terminar		**m** cerrar	
d vender		**n** empujar	
e escuchar		**o** tirar	
f perder		**p** olvidar	
g escoger		**q** salir	
h esperar		**r** entrar	
i organizar		**s** oír	
j invitar		**t** partir	

II What did Marcos do this morning? Add the correct past participle.

a He _____ al tenis con Jaime. (jugar) — I played tennis with Jaime.

b Luego he _____ un café con mi mujer. (tomar) — Then I had a coffee with my wife.

c Después he _____ a mi colega Juan. (llamar) — Next I rang my colleague Juan.

d Hemos _____ del nuevo proyecto. (hablar) — We talked about the new plan.

e Me ha _____ su cooperación. (asegurar) — He assured me of his cooperation.

f Hemos _____ una fecha para la rueda de prensa. (decidir) — We decided on a date for the press conference.

g Me ha _____ el nuevo folleto por e-mail. (enviar) — He sent me the new brochure by e-mail.

h He _____ una página. (cambiar) — I changed a page.

i Yo la he ____. (imprimir)   I printed it out.

j Después he ____ una   After that I watched a soap on
telenovela. (mirar)   TV.

B Irregular past participles

Many English past participles are irregular, but we are so used to them that we don't notice them:

run → run; eat → eaten; drink → drunk, etc.

Some Spanish verbs also have irregular past participles. Although there seem to be quite a lot, they are easy to learn, as groups of them follow the same patterns.

Here are the most important irregular past participles. Remember that the examples can be translated as, for example *I have opened* or *I opened*.

infinitive	past participle	example	meaning	similar
abrir	abierto	he abierto la puerta	I have opened the door	
cubrir	cubierto	ha cubierto la sartén	he covered the frying pan	descubrir
decir	dicho	no hemos dicho nada	we have said nothing	
hacer	hecho	has hecho algo malo	you did something bad	satisfacer
volver	vuelto	no han vuelto aún	they have not returned yet	devolver, etc.
escribir	escrito	ha escrito una carta	he has written a letter	describir
freír	frito	he frito una tortilla	I have fried an omelette	
morir	muerto	mi tío ha muerto	my uncle has died	
poner	puesto	se ha puesto un collar	she put on a necklace	componer, etc.
ver	visto	no la he visto hoy	I haven't seen her today	
romper	roto	usted ha roto la llave	you have broken the key	

Note: many of these have 'compound' forms, not just those shown. Keep your eyes open!

III Complete these sentences by adding the past participle of the verb given in brackets.

a Este cliente ha ____ el nuevo folleto. (ver) — This customer has seen the new brochure.

b Hemos ____ el texto. (escribir) — We wrote the text.

c Paqui lo ha ____ en el ordenador. (poner) — Paqui put it on the computer.

d La casa FoCo ha ____ esta versión. (hacer) — The FoCo company made this version.

e El cliente ha ____ que le gusta. (decir) — The customer said he liked it.

f Ha ____ a firmar el contrato. (volver) — He signed the contract again.

IV Now tell the story of Manuel's car. Complete these sentences using the perfect tense of the verb given in brackets. Not all the past participles are irregular!

a Manuel ____ 100.000 euros en la lotería. (ganar) — Manuel won 100,000 euros in the lottery.

b ____ comprar un coche nuevo para su mujer. (querer) — He wanted to buy a new car for his wife.

c ____ un anuncio para un coche eléctrico. (ver) — He saw an advert for an electric car.

d ____ el coche. (comprar) — He bought the car.

e El coche no le ____ a su mujer y ____ venderlo. (gustar, decidir) — His wife didn't like the car and she decided to sell it.

f ____ un anuncio en el periódico. (poner) — She put an advertisement in the newspaper.

g Un amigo de su marido ____ una cita para probar el coche. (hacer) — A friend of her husband made an appointment to try out the car.

h Manuel ____ a su mujer con su amigo en el coche. (ver) — Manuel saw his wife in the car with his friend.

i ____ que tenían una aventura. (creer) — He thought they were having an affair.

j ____ el coche. (seguir) — He followed the car.

k ____ el límite de velocidad. (exceder) — He went too fast.

l La Guardia Civil lo ____. (detener) — The police stopped him.

m ____ que pagar una multa. (tener) — He had to pay a fine.

V Now can you translate these?

  a Sofía has read his latest novel. (su última novela)
  b Have you read the book?
  c We haven't read the book.
  d They have seen the film of the book.
  e Sofía saw the film yesterday.
  f We haven't seen the film yet.
  g Have you seen the film?

Checklist: past participles

Most participles end in **-ado** or **-ido**.

Regular verbs:

-ar verbs end in **-ado**
-er and **-ir** verbs end in **-ido**

Many of the most commonly-used verbs have irregular past
participles. Look for patterns to try to remember them:

abierto, cubierto; dicho, hecho; escrito, frito; puesto, visto

1.4.3 Reflexive verbs in the perfect tense

Reflexive verbs behave in the same way in the perfect tense
as they do in the present tense, with the reflexive pronoun
coming before the appropriate part of the verb **haber**.

present	perfect
me levanto	me he levantado
te levantas	te has levantado
se levanta	se ha levantado
nos levantamos	nos hemos levantado
os levantáis	os habéis levantado
se levantan	se han levantado

At first you will probably only need to use reflexive verbs in the first
person, so learn one phrase by heart and use it as a model to
make other phrases later.

Me he levantado temprano.	I got up early.
Me he paseado en el parque.	I went for a walk in the park.
Me he perdido.	I got lost.
Me he dirigido a casa.	I headed for home.

I For more practice with the other persons, see if you can give the correct form of the perfect tense of **levantarse** to complete these sentences. When did they get up?

a Esta mañana, yo ____ a las seis.
b El panadero ____ a las cuatro.
c Su mujer ____ a las cuatro y media.
d Gil ____ a las siete y media.
e Patricio y Mónica ____ a las siete menos cuarto.
f Celia, ¿a qué hora ____ ?
g Nosotros ____ a las seis.
h Los señores Pérez ____ a las nueve.
i Amelia y Carmen ____ a las nueve y media.
j ¿A qué hora ____ tú esta mañana?

Here are some more reflexive verbs. You probably know most of them already.

infinitive	meaning	present tense	perfect tense
acordarse	to remember	me acuerdo	me he acordado
acostarse	to go to bed	me acuesto	me he acostado
afeitarse	to shave	me afeito	me he afeitado
arreglarse	to get ready	me arreglo	me he arreglado
despertarse	to wake up	me despierto	me he despertado
dormirse	to fall asleep	me duermo	me he dormido
enfadarse	to get angry	me enfado	me he enfadado
equivocarse	to make a mistake	me equivoco	me he equivocado
lavarse	to wash	me lavo	me he lavado
pasearse	to go for a walk	me paseo	me he paseado
peinarse	to comb one's hair	me peino	me he peinado
perderse	to get lost	me pierdo	me he perdido

Checklist: perfect tense

You use the perfect tense to talk about something which has happened at a recent specific time in the past.

All verbs form the perfect tense with **haber** and the past participle of the verb, e.g. **he comido**.

haber: he, has, ha, hemos, habéis, han

The past participle does not change its ending when used to form the perfect tense.

1.4.4 When to use the imperfect tense

▶▶ **If you know when to use the imperfect tense, go on to 1.4.5.**

You use the imperfect tense to:

- describe what something was like in the past:

When I was small, we lived in Scotland.	Cuando era pequeño vivíamos en Escocia.
The house was old.	La casa era vieja.
It rained every day.	Llovía todos los días.

- say what someone or something used to do:

I used to walk to school.	Iba a la escuela a pie.
We used to collect wood for the fire.	Recogíamos leña para el fuego.
My father used to go fishing.	Mi padre iba de pesca.

- describe an interrupted action (say what someone/ something was doing when something else happened):

I was watching television when the phone rang.	Veía (imperfect) la televisión cuando sonó (preterite) el teléfono.

If you would use *was* or *were* or *used to* in English, you need to use the imperfect to say the same thing in Spanish.

The imperfect is usually the tense to use for describing the weather in the past.

hacía sol – it was sunny	llovía – it was raining

1.4.5 How to form the imperfect tense

▶▶ **If you know how to form the imperfect tense, go on to 1.4.7.**

To form the imperfect tense, you need to know the infinitive stem (e.g. **hablar → habl-**) and add the endings for **-ar** verbs or **-er** and **-ir** verbs as appropriate.

person	endings for -ar verbs	endings for -er and -ir verbs
yo	-aba	-ía
tú	-abas	-ías
él/ella/usted	-aba	-ía
nosotros/as	-ábamos	-íamos
vosotros/as	-abais	-íais
ellos/ellas/ustedes	-aban	-ían

A Regular verbs

Here are full examples of the different types of regular verbs:

hablar	comer	vivir
habl**aba**	com**ía**	viv**ía**
habl**abas**	com**ías**	viv**ías**
habl**aba**	com**ía**	viv**ía**
habl**ábamos**	com**íamos**	viv**íamos**
habl**abais**	com**íais**	viv**íais**
habl**aban**	com**ían**	viv**ían**

I   What were they doing when the lights went out?

a Mi marido _____ delante de la televisión. (dormir)
b Carlos _____ la televisión. (mirar)
c Maleni _____ una revista. (leer)
d Yo _____ con mi vecina. (charlar)
e (Nosotros) _____ del nuevo primer ministro. (hablar)
f Sarita se _____ (duchar)
g Francisco _____ a su novia. (telefonear)
h Andrés y su amiga _____ sus motos en la cochera. (reparar)
i Nicolás y Alejandro _____ al billar en la sala de juegos. (jugar)

B Irregular verbs

The following three verbs are irregular in the imperfect tense, but note that the endings are similar to those of regular verbs:

ser	ir	ver
era	iba	veía
eras	ibas	veías
era	iba	veía
éramos	íbamos	veíamos
erais	ibais	veíais
eran	iban	veían

II Give the correct imperfect form of **ser** or **ir**.

  a She was very small.   _____ muy pequeña.
  b They were going to school.   _____ al colegio.
  c We were young.   _____ jóvenes.
  d You were a clever child.   _____ un niño inteligente.
  e I used to go to the shops.   _____ a las tiendas.

III Give the correct imperfect form of the verb in brackets.

  a (Yo) ____ en la parada del autobús. (esperar)
  b (Tú) ____ Hevia en tu walkman. (escuchar)
  c (Nosotros) ____ al pueblo. (ir)
  d Patricio ____ el periódico. (leer)
  e (Ella) ____ a su novio. (esperar)
  f Martín ____ de su casa. (salir)
  g Sus padres ____ en el campo. (estar)
  h Silvia ____ footing. (hacer)
  i Vosotros ____ la televisión. (ver)
  j Mi padre ____ un aperitivo. (beber)

IV Complete the sentences to describe what the weather was like.

  a ____ buen tiempo. (hacer)
  b ____ (nevar)
  c ____ sol. (hacer)
  d El viento ____ (soplar)
  e El sol ____ (brillar)
  f ____ (llover)
  g La niebla ____ (desaparecer)
  h ____ calor. (hacer)
  i ____ una tormenta. (haber)
  j El mar ____ agitado. (estar)

V In the old days ...

  a Cuando mi bisabuelo ____ pequeño, ____ en el campo. (ser, vivir)
  b Las casas ____ construidas de piedra. (estar)
  c ____ menos de veinte habitantes en su pueblo. (haber)
  d Se ____ la viña. (cultivar)
  e Los niños ____ en los campos. (trabajar)
  f ____ las uvas. (recoger)
  g Sus padres ____ el vino. (hacer)
  h No ____ electricidad. (haber)
  i Su madre ____ en un fuego de leña. (cocinar)
  j Mi bisabuelo ____ que ir a pie. (tener)
  k Para ir a la escuela, ____ una hora andando. (tardar)

C Reflexive verb

Reflexive verbs behave the same in the imperfect tense as they do in the present tense, with the reflexive pronoun coming before the appropriate person of the verb, so they present no problems.

VI Complete these sentences with the appropriate form of the reflexive verbs in brackets.

a Cuando era joven, yo ____ a las siete. (levantarse)
b Luego ____ en el cuarto de baño. (ducharse)
c ____ antes de tomar el desayuno. (vestirse)
d Después, ____ los dientes. (lavarse)
e Luego ____ en el espejo antes de ir al colegio. (mirarse)
f Mi hermano perezoso ____ a las ocho. (levantarse)
g No ____ casi nunca. (ducharse)
h Sólo ____ antes de salir. (vestirse)
i Nosotros dos, ____ prisa para llegar al cole a tiempo. (darse)
j Mis padres siempre ____ antes que yo. (despertarse)
k Nuestros padres ____ mucho con mi hermano. (enfadarse)
l Durante el día, mi abuela ____ en el parque. (pasearse)

1.4.6 Checklist: imperfect tense

The imperfect tense is easy as it is always formed in the same way.

- Take the infinitive of the verb, remove the **-ar/-er/-ir** and add the new endings.
- There are just three irregular verbs: **ser (era), ir (iba)** and **ver (veía)**.
- The endings for **-ar** verbs are: **-aba, -abas, -aba, -ábamos, -abais, -aban**; and for **-er** and **-ir** verbs are: **-ía, -ías, -ía, -íamos, -íais, -ían**.

You are most likely to need to use the imperfect tense when talking about yourself, or about the weather: **hacía** ..., **había** ..., etc.

1.4.7 The preterite tense

 **If you know how to form the preterite tense, go on to 1.4.10.**

The preterite tense in Spanish is just like the English past simple tense, consisting of just one word. It is always used to describe a single, completed action, unless the action has just happened, in which case the perfect tense would be needed. The preterite is therefore used for narrative and reports of past events, as well as for recent everyday events.

English verb	English past simple	Spanish verb	Spanish preterite
to speak	I spoke	hablar	hablé
to eat	I ate	comer	comí
to live	I lived	vivir	viví

In Spanish, most verbs form the preterite on a stem based on the infinitive minus **-ar/-er/-ir**. To get used to the sound of the preterite, choose one of the phrases below, or make up one of your own, and practise saying it until you are really fluent. The following examples could be expressed in the perfect tense if recent actions, but are more likely to be in the preterite.

Fui al bar y pedí una cerveza.	I went to the bar and I ordered a beer.
Perdiste un cuchillo y rompiste una taza.	You lost a knife and broke a cup.
Fue al pueblo e hizo las compras.	He/She went to town and did some shopping.
Fuimos a la estación y cogimos el tren de las seis.	We went to the station and got the 6 o'clock train.
Olvidasteis las llaves y abandonasteis el coche.	You forgot the keys and abandoned the car.
Fueron al mercado y compraron peras.	They went to the market and bought pears.

A Regular verbs

Here are the preterite forms of regular **-ar**, **-er** and **-ir** verbs. Note that **-er** and **-ir** verbs share the same endings.

-ar: hablar	-er: comer	-ir: vivir
habl**é**	com**í**	viv**í**
habl**aste**	com**iste**	viv**iste**
habl**ó**	com**ió**	viv**ió**
habl**amos**	com**imos**	viv**imos**
habl**asteis**	com**isteis**	viv**isteis**
habl**aron**	com**ieron**	viv**ieron**

I Practise with the following. How would you say ...?

a I spoke
b you spoke (tú)
c she spoke
d they spoke
e you ate (ustedes)

f we ate
g Did you eat? (vosotros)
h John lived
i you lived (usted)
j my wife and I lived

II What did Marcos do yesterday? Put the verb given in brackets into the right form of the preterite.

a ____ con mi amigo Jaime. (charlar) — I chatted to my friend Jaime.

b Luego ____ un café con mi mujer. (tomar) — Then I had a coffee with my wife.

c Después ____ a mi colega Juan. (llamar) — Next I rang my colleague Juan.

d ____ del nuevo proyecto. (hablar) — We talked about the new plan.

e Me ____ su cooperación. (asegurar) — He assured me of his cooperation.

f ____ una fecha para la rueda de prensa. (decidir) — We decided on a date for the press conference.

g Me ____ el nuevo folleto por e-mail. (enviar) — He sent me the new brochure by e-mail.

h ____ una página. (cambiar) — I changed a page.

i Yo la ____ (imprimir) — I printed it out.

j Después ____ una telenovela. (mirar) — After that I watched a soap on TV.

B Verbs with spelling and stem changes

A number of verbs need a spelling change in the **yo** form of the preterite to keep the sound correct. Here are examples of the main changes:

-c- → -qu-	-g- → -gu-	-z- → -c-
busqu**é**	jugu**é**	cruc**é**
busc**aste**, etc.	jug**aste**, etc.	cruz**aste**, etc.

III What did Marcos do last Saturday? Add the right form of the preterite.

a ____ al tenis con Jaime. (jugar) — I played tennis with Jaime.

b Después ____ la ciudad. (cruzar) — Next I crossed the city.

c Luego ____ a mi mujer en la tienda. (buscar) — I looked for my wife in the shop.

d ____ un sofá nuevo. (buscar) — We looked for a new sofa.

e ____ la plaza para ir al parque. (cruzar) — We crossed the square to go to the park.

f Allí nos ____ nuestros hijos. (buscar)

Our children looked for us there.

g Nuestro hijo ____ al fútbol. (jugar)

Our son played football.

h Nuestras hijas ____ al baloncesto. (jugar)

Our daughters played basketball.

A few verbs have a spelling change in the third person singular and plural forms: in the case of **creer** and **leer**, the -i- changes to -y- in these forms. A handful of -ir verbs with stem changes in the present tense change -e- to -i- or -o- to -u- in the third person forms. Note that this is the only example of stem-changing in the preterite. The rest of the changes seen in the present tense form are not needed, since, for almost all verbs in the preterite, the stress is always on the ending.

Here are these two types of change presented together:

-i- → -y-	-e- → -i-	-o- → -u-
creer	**preferir**	**dormir**
creí	preferí	dormí
creíste	preferiste	dormiste
cre**y**ó	pref**i**rió	d**u**rmió
creímos	preferimos	dormimos
creísteis	preferisteis	dormisteis
cre**y**eron	pref**i**rieron	d**u**rmieron

C   Irregular verbs

Here are the only completely irregular verbs in the preterite tense. Note that **ser** and **ir** actually share the same preterite forms – weird but wonderful, as it saves learning an extra set of forms!

dar – to give	ver – to see	ir – to go + ser – to be
di	vi	fui
diste	viste	fuiste
dio	vio	fue
dimos	vimos	fuimos
disteis	visteis	fuisteis
dieron	vieron	fueron

IV   Who watched Real Madrid v Barcelona? Complete these sentences by adding the right form of **dar, ir** or **ver**.

a Mi tío me ____ un billete para el partido.

b Los padres de Paco le ____ un billete también.

c Los dos ____ al partido en metro.
d Primero yo ____ a comprar una camisa del Real.
e Mi amigo Paco ____ a comprar una camisa del Barça.
f Al salir de la tienda, yo ____ a Paco con su camisa.
g No ____ al partido con Paco.
h No ____ el partido juntos.

There is a small group of verbs which don't fit the patterns above, and which all have an irregular preterite stem: these are known as the **pretérito grave**, which means their stress is always on the last-but-one syllable, which is why there are no accents on any of the forms. There is just one set of endings which are a sort of blend of the preterite endings for **-ar** and **-er/-ir** verbs: **-e, -iste, -o, -imos, -isteis, -ieron**.

Here is an example, followed by a list of the most useful **pretérito grave** verbs:

estar – to be   estuve, estuviste, estuvo, estuvimos, estuvisteis, estuvieron

infinitive	meaning	preterite stem	preterite
andar	to walk	anduv-	anduv**e**, etc.
poder	to be able to	pud-	pud**e**
poner	to put	pus-	pus**e**
querer	to want	quis-	quis**e**
saber	to know	sup-	sup**e**
tener	to have	tuv-	tuv**e**
venir	to come	vin-	vin**e**

One verb also has a spelling change in the third person singular:

infinitive	meaning	stem	preterite
hacer	to do, make	hic-, hiz-	hice, hiciste, hi**z**o, hicimos, hicisteis, hicieron

Two or three verbs have these forms except that they lose the **-i-** in the third person plural. The most useful one is:

infinitive	meaning	stem	preterite
decir	to say	dij-	dije, dijiste, dijo, dijimos, dijisteis, dij**eron**

Although these look awkward, they are easy to learn; try to learn the stems by heart – some even sound rather amusing.

V Storytelling in the preterite: complete by adding the correct form of the right verb from the list in the box below.

El año pasado, (nosotros) __1__ a España. Nos __2__ dos semanas en la playa. __ 3__ un apartamento en Tarifa. Mi novio __ 4__ windsurf y yo __ 5__ todo el día tomando el sol en la playa y leyendo.

Mi hermano y su novia __ 6__ a quedarse un fin de semana con nosotros. Nos __ 7__ mucho. Por la tarde __ 8__ en un restaurante y luego __9__ hasta las tres de la madrugada. Al día siguiente, todos __10__ windsurf. Y vosotros, ¿adónde __ 11__ y qué __ 12__ allí?

> alquilar, bailar, cenar, divertir(se), hacer (x 3), ir (x 2), pasar, quedarse, venir

D Reflexive verbs

Reflexive verbs behave in the same way in the preterite tense as they do in the present, with the reflexive pronoun coming before the appropriate person of the verb, so they present no problems.

VI What did we do yesterday? Add the right form of the verb given in brackets.

a ____ a las ocho. (despertarse)
b ____ a las nueve. (levantarse)
c ____ a la orilla del río. (pasearse)
d ____ de camino. (equivocarse)
e ____ (perderse)
f ____ en un pequeño pueblo. (pararse)
g Mi amiga ____ nerviosa. (ponerse)
h (Ella) ____ de un amigo que vive allí cerca. (acordarse)
i (Ella) ____, dejándome solo. (irse)

1.4.8 Checklist: preterite tense

You use the preterite tense to talk about a single, completed action which happened at a specific time in the past.

- Almost all verbs have regular endings, but some need minor spelling changes.
- The endings for **-ar** verbs are: **-é, -aste, -ó, -amos, -asteis, -aron.**

- The endings for both **-er** and **-ir** verbs are: **-í, -iste, -ió, -imos, -isteis, -ieron**.
- A group of verbs have special stems, and the endings: **-e, -iste, -o, -imos, -isteis, -ieron**.

1.4.9 Preterite or imperfect?

Remember to use the imperfect tense for the action that was ongoing, and the preterite tense for the action that 'interrupted' it.

I You need to use both the imperfect and the preterite to complete these sentences.

a Sus padres ____ (vivir) en León cuando Nuria ____ (nacer).
b Cuando ella ____ (ser) pequeña, su familia ____ (mudarse) a Perú.
c Nuria ____ (tener) cinco años cuando su hermano ____ (nacer).
d Pepe ____ (sufrir) un accidente cuando ____ (tener) diez años.
e ____ (cruzar) la calle cuando un coche no ____ (pararse) en el semáforo.
f Nuria ____ (ver) el accidente mientras ____ (esperar) el autobús.
g Ella ____ (tener) diecinueve años cuando ____ (pasar) su examen de selectividad.
h Nuria ____ (estudiar) biología cuando ____ (decidir) abandonar sus estudios.
i ____ (hacer) un cursillo de informática cuando ____ (ver) el anuncio de MegaSA.
j Ella ____ (trabajar) en esta empresa cuando ____ (conocer) a su futuro marido.
k Nuria ____ (ser) jefe de personal cuando él ____ (solicitar) un empleo.
l ____ (hacer) buen tiempo cuando Nuria y José ____ (casarse).

1.4.10 ▶Fast track: The past tenses

There are different ways of saying what has happened in the past.

The perfect tense

This is used to describe an action in the past which has been completed recently.

The perfect tense is not used as often as in English. The preterite is often used in its place.

The perfect tense is made up of the 'auxiliary' or 'helper' verb **haber** and the past participle, as in English: *I have eaten* – **he comido**.

Past participles do not change their spelling when used as part of a perfect-tense verb.

The imperfect tense

The imperfect is used to talk about an ongoing or habitual action in the past.

If you can use *was/were* or *used to* in English, you use the imperfect tense in Spanish.

It is formed by adding to the infinitive stem the endings: **-aba, -abas, -aba, -ábamos, -abais, -aban** for **-ar** verbs, and **-ía, -ías, -ía, -íamos, -íais, -ían** for **-er** and **-ir** verbs.

The preterite tense

This is used to describe a single, completed action in the past. It is often used where we might expect the perfect tense.

For **-ar** verbs, take the **-ar** off the infinitive and add the following endings to the stem: **-é, -aste, -ó, -amos, -asteis, -aron**.

For **-er/-ir** verbs add: **-í, -iste, -ió, -imos, -isteis, -ieron**.

A few verbs need a minor spelling change, and a small group have special stems and endings.

1.5 The future tenses and the conditional

You use the future tense to talk about something that is going to happen, or something you want to do or are going to do in the future. In Spanish, just as in English, there are two ways of saying what is going to happen. Note also that the present tense is often used to express an event which will happen in the near future (see 1.2).

A The near future/the future immediate: *el futuro inmediato*

This is like the English *I am going to ...*, e.g. *I am going to go, He is going to play*, and is made up of **ir** (*to go*) + **a** + the infinitive of the main verb:

Voy a salir.   I am going to go out.

This is the most useful future tense to learn, as it is the one used most frequently in conversation when talking about the near future: this evening, tomorrow, in the next few days or when you would use *going to* in English.

B The future simple: *el futuro*

This is the 'proper' future tense. It translates the English *will* and can imply intention as well as future action, e.g. *He will go – I will make sure he does!*

jugaré	I will play
irá	he will go
escucharán	they will listen

 The future tense is easier to use if you are listing a lot of things that you are going to do or that will happen, rather than repeat **ir a** several times.

C The conditional: *el condicional*

This is not strictly considered a future tense but it talks about the future: what you would do if ...

It translates *would/should/could* in English: *I would like to go if ...*, talking about something you would like to do in the future.

I would like to go to Madrid.
We really should/ought to go.
Could we go tomorrow?

It is also used as a polite way of stating a wish or asking for something:

I would like to leave now.   Me gustaría irme ahora.

1.5.1 The near future/future immediate: I am going to ...

▶▶ **If you know all about the future immediate, go on to 1.5.2.**

To make the future immediate, you need to know the present tense of the verb **ir** and the infinitive of the verb you want to use.

Here is the present tense of **ir**:

singular	meaning	plural	meaning
voy	I am going	vamos	we are going
vas	you are going	vais	you are going
va	he/she is going/ you are going	van	they are going/you are going

Voy a cenar en casa.	I am going to have dinner at home.
Tú vas a ver el programa.	You are going to watch the programme.
Ella va a llegar tarde.	She is going to arrive late.
Nosotros vamos a almorzar.	We are going to have lunch.
Vosotros vais a visitar el museo.	You are going to visit the museum.
Ellos van a esquiar.	They are going to go skiing.

I What are these people going to do? Complete the sentences by adding the correct form of the verb **ir**.

a Yo ____ a hacer windsurf.
b Tú ____ a hacer ala delta.
c Mario ____ a hacer rafting.
d Usted ____ a hacer surfing.
e Nosotros ____ a comprar un todoterreno.
f Vosotros ____ a esquiar.
g Natalia y Simón ____ a hacer snowboard.
h ¿Ustedes ____ a hacer alpinismo?
i Patricio y Benjamín ____ a hacer espeleología.
j Yo me ____ a quedar en casa.

II What are they going to do for Diego's birthday? Add the missing part of **ir**.

a Sus colegas ____ a organizar una fiesta.
b Tomás ____ a hacer un pastel.
c Sabina ____ a enviar las invitaciones.
d Isabel y Silvia ____ a preparar las tapas.
e Sergio ____ a comprar una botella de Cava.
f Su jefe ____ a ofrecerle un regalo.
g Roldán ____ a decorar la habitación.
h Nosotros ____ a ayudar a Roldán.
i Silvia ____ a buscar los vasos.
j Vosotros ____ a cantar «cumpleaños feliz».

If you know about the future tense, go on to 1.5.3.

This is the 'proper' future tense, sometimes called the future simple because it consists of just one word. It translates the English *will* and is used to talk about events which will take place in the future.

jugaré	I will play
irá	he will go
escucharán	they will listen

A   Regular verbs

Fortunately, most verbs are regular in the future tense! It is made by adding these endings to the infinitive: **-é, -ás, -á, -emos, -éis, -án**. A few verbs have a slighly modified future stem.

 Notice that the endings are the same as those of the present tense of the verb **haber** (but without the **-ab-** in the **vosotros** form).

Here are examples of regular verbs in full:

-ar verbs	-er verbs	-ir verbs
hablar**é**	comer**é**	vivir**é**
hablar**ás**	comer**ás**	vivir**ás**
hablar**á**	comer**á**	vivir**á**
hablar**emos**	comer**emos**	vivir**emos**
hablar**éis**	comer**éis**	vivir**éis**
hablar**án**	comer**án**	vivir**án**

I   Give the correct future tense forms of the verbs in brackets.

a nosotros ____ (mirar)
b tú ____ (preparar)
c vosotros ____ (meter)
d ellos ____ (comer)
e usted ____ (permitir)

f él ____ (escribir)
g ellas ____ (llegar)
h nosotros ____ (entrar)
i yo ____ (partir)
j ustedes ____ (subir)

II   What are they going to wear for the fiesta? Add the correct form of **llevar**.

a Yo ____ el traje tradicional de la región.
b Julieta ____ una falda roja y una blusa blanca.

c Mi amigo _____ su traje negro y una camisa blanca.
d Nicolás _____ sus vaqueros y una camiseta vieja, como siempre.
e Mis amigas _____ su vestido tradicional bordado.
f Mis amigos _____ un pantalón negro y una camisa azul.
g Nosotros _____ unos calcetines blancos y unos zapatos negros.
h Y usted, ¿qué _____?
i ¿Qué _____ tú?

B   Irregular verbs
Some of the most common verbs are irregular in the future tense.

 Look for patterns to help you remember them. Choose the four that you think you are most likely to need, and learn the **yo** form.

Here are the most useful verbs with irregular future forms. Notice that it is the stem that is slightly irregular – the endings are all regular:

infinitive	future
decir	diré, dirás, etc.
haber	habré
hacer	haré
poder	podré
poner	pondré
querer	querré
saber	sabré
salir	saldré
tener	tendré
venir	vendré

NB: Any compounds based on the verbs above have the same irregularity in the future tense.

 Useful expressions: **ya te lo diré** – *I'll tell you soon;* **hará falta** – *it will be necessary*

III   For more practice, give the correct form of the verb in brackets.

a yo _____ (tener)
b vosotros _____ (venir)
c tú _____ (hacer)
d nosotros _____ (haber)

e él ____ (salir)
f ella ____ (saber)
g ustedes ____ (querer)
h nosotros ____ (decir)
i vosotros ____ (poner)
j ellos ____ (poder)
k usted ____ (tener)
l yo ____ (venir)

IV   Write in the correct future form of the verb in brackets.

a El año que viene, yo ____ veinte años. (tener)
b En este momento, estudio en España, pero el año que viene yo ____ a Inglaterra. (ir)
c Yo ____ un cursillo de inglés en Oxford. (hacer)
d (Yo) te ____ mi nueva dirección. (enviar)
e Tú ____ a verme en Oxford, ¿verdad? (ir)
f Pues, tú ____ , y nosotros ____ a Londres juntos. (venir, ir)
g También ____ hacer un viaje a Escocia, pero ____ necesario ir en coche porque ir en tren ____ demasiado dinero! (poder, ser, costar)
h Al terminar mi curso, yo ____ a España, y ____ para mi padre en su oficina. (volver, trabajar).

V   Before leaving for a holiday in the Sierra Nevada, a couple goes over the travel arrangements with the travel agent. Add the correct future form of the verb in brackets.

a ¿Cuándo ____ nosotros? (salir)
b Ustedes ____ el vuelo de Iberia de las 14h50. (coger)
c Un autobús les ____ al llegar y les ____ al hotel. (esperar, llevar)
d Todo el mundo ____ esquiar. (poder)
e A mediodía, ustedes ____ en el hotel o en un bar, como quieran. (comer)
f Por la tarde, ____ salir. (poder)
g Como ____ frío, ustedes ____ que llevar ropa adecuada. (hacer, tener)

1.5.3   The conditional: I would ...

▶▶ **If you don't want to practise the conditional, go on to the Fast track (1.5.4), as you might need to be able to recognise it when you hear it.**

> You probably already know the expression **me gustaría** – *I would like.*

The conditional is used to translate *would, could* and *should* in English. It is called the conditional because you use it

when you are making a condition: *I would go if you paid me!*
But it is also used to be polite: *I would like a box of chocolates.*

A Regular verbs

The conditional is easy to learn as it is very similar to the
future tense: infinitive + one set of endings. The endings
are the same as the imperfect endings for **-er/-ir** verbs: **-ía**,
-ías, -ía, -íamos, -íais, -ían.

-ar verbs	-er verbs	-ir verbs
hablar**ía**	comer**ía**	vivir**ía**
hablar**ías**	comer**ías**	vivir**ías**
hablar**ía**	comer**ía**	vivir**ía**
hablar**íamos**	comer**íamos**	vivir**íamos**
hablar**íais**	comer**íais**	vivir**íais**
hablar**ían**	comer**ían**	vivir**ían**

VI How would you say the following?

I would ...

a eat (comer)
b drink (beber)
c sleep (dormir)
d speak (hablar)
e live (vivir)
f buy (comprar)
g ask (pedir)
h listen (escuchar)
i watch (mirar)

VII Add the right conditional form of **jugar** to the following.

a Yo ____ al tenis.   I would play tennis.
b Mi amiga ____ también.   My friend would play too.
c Sus amigas ____ también.   Her friends would play too.
d Nosotros no ____   We wouldn't play.
e Vosotros ____ al voleibol.   You would play volleyball.

VIII Add the right conditional form of **preferir** to these
sentences.

a Yo ____ ir a la playa.   I would prefer to go to the
                                           beach.
b Mi novio ____ hacer windsurf.   My boyfriend would prefer to go
                                           windsurfing.
c Mis amigas ____ ir al pueblo.   My girlfriends would prefer to go
                                           to town.

d Nosotros ＿＿ comer en un restaurante. — We would prefer to eat in a restaurant.

e ¿Qué ＿＿ usted hacer? — What would you prefer?

IX **Gustar** and other 'back-to-front verbs'. Add the right conditional form of each one, and the correct pronoun (see 3.3).

a ＿＿ salir. (gustar) — I would like to go out.

b A Gil ＿＿ quedarse en casa. (apetecer) — Gil would feel like staying in.

c A Patricia ＿＿ ir al cine. (encantar) — Patricia would love to go to the cinema.

d A mis padres ＿＿ ir a Chile. (interesar) — My parents would be interested in going to Chile.

e ¿Qué ＿＿ hacer, Paqui? (apetecer) — What would you feel like doing, Paqui?

f ¿Qué ＿＿ hacer, niños? (gustar) — What would you like to do, children?

g ¿Qué ＿＿ hacer, Señor Pérez? (gustar) — What would you like to do, Señor Pérez?

h ¿Qué ＿＿ hacer, señores? (gustar) — What would you like to do, ladies and gentlemen?

B Irregular verbs

These have the same stems as in the future tense (see 1.5.2 B), but with the regular conditional endings.

infinitive	conditional
decir	diría
haber	habría
hacer	haría
poder	podría
poner	pondría
querer	querría
saber	sabría
salir	saldría
tener	tendría
venir	vendría

X Talking about yourself: how would you say the following?

a Yo ＿＿ algo para comer. (hacer) — I would make something to eat.

b ＿＿ del pueblo. (salir) — I would leave town.

c ＿＿ un amigo. (tener) — I would have a friend.

d Se lo ＿＿ a mis amigos. (decir) — I would tell my friends.

e ____ a España. (venir) I would come to Spain.
f ____ hacer windsurf. (poder) I could windsurf.
g Me ____ un abrigo. (ponerse) I would put on a coat.
h ____ la respuesta. (saber) I would know the answer.
i Yo ____ salir. (querer) I would want to go out.
j Yo le ____ escrito. (haber) I would have written to him.

XI What could they do? Fill in the correct form of **poder**.

a Nuria ____ regresar a casa. Nuria could go home.
b Nosotros ____ ir al cine. We could go to the cinema.
c ____ ir al polideportivo. We could go to the leisure centre.
d Yo ____ hacer judo. I could do judo.
e Tú ____ jugar al voleibol. You could play volleyball.
f Carmen ____ hacer equitación. Carmen could go riding.
g Los niños ____ ir a la piscina. The children could go swimming.
h ____ reunirnos después. We could meet afterwards.
i ____ir a la bodega. We could go to the bodega.
j ____ir a mi casa. We could go back to my house.

1.5.4 ▶Fast track: Future and conditional

D The future tenses

There are two ways of saying what you are going to do or what is going to happen.

- The future immediate, or near future, is like the English *going to*. It is made up of the verb *to go* (**ir: voy, vas, va, vamos, vais, van**) + **a** + the infinitive.
- The future simple tense is made up of the infinitive and the endings: **-é, -ás, -á, -emos, -éis, -án**.

The pattern of the endings is like those of the present tense of **haber** without the **-ab-** in the **vosotros/as** form.

If you can't manage learning both ways at the moment, concentrate on the *future immediate*, but you should be able to recognise the future simple when someone uses it.

The two forms are often interchangeable.

- The *future immediate* is used more than the future simple in conversation when describing plans for the immediate future.

- If you would use *going to* in English, use **ir** + **a** + infinitive in Spanish.
- It is used for something that is about to happen:

Ella va a casarse con Pablo.   She is going to marry Pablo (she is engaged).

- The *future simple* is sometimes used for something that you expect to happen.
- It is also used in lists where repeating **ir** + **a** + infinitive would be clumsy to say.
- It can be used to talk about something that 'may' happen:

Ella se casará con Pablo.   She will marry Pablo, one day, eventually . . .

These are the verbs most commonly used future tense, some of which have an irregular stem. It is useful to be able to recognise which verb they come from:

iré	ir
tendré	tener
deberé	deber
seré	ser
haré	hacer
podré	poder
cogeré	coger
sabré	saber
vendré	venir
veré	ver
querré	querer

D   The conditional

The conditional translates *would*, e.g. *I would go, I would like.*

- You probably already know **me gustaría** (*I would like*), so you already know one ending. The endings are: **-ía, -ías, -ía, -íamos, -íais, -ían.**
- The most useful conditionals are:

me gustaría	I would like
me encantaría	I would love
preferiría	I would prefer
podríamos	we could
deberíamos	we should, ought to
sería	it would be

1.6 The subjunctive

▶▶ **If you are not ready for the subjunctive yet, go on to 1.7. If you just want to check your knowledge go to 1.6.4 Fast track.**

The subjunctive is not used much in English any more (only in expressions such as *If I were you ...*), but it has to be used in many expressions in Spanish. You are not likely to need to use those expressions yourself very often, other than the forms used for imperatives (see 1.3.3 C and D), but it is useful to be able to recognise them when you hear them and to understand which verb is being used. Choose one or two of the expressions to learn by heart and then use them as a model.

If you want to know more about the subjunctive go to *¡Acción Gramática!* or *¡Viva la Gramática!* (P. Turk and M. Zollo).

The subjunctive is nearly always preceded by the word **que**, but this does not mean that **que** is always followed by the subjunctive!

In Spanish, the subjunctive is used after verbs which express a wish or desire:

Me gustaría que se vaya.	I would like him to go.
Espero que venga.	I hope that she will come.

... or a requirement (after **es necesario/hace falta** – *it is necessary that*):

Hace falta que sepa conducir.	He must be able to drive.

... or a doubt or uncertainty:

No creo que tenga dinero.	I don't think (that) she has any money.
Es posible que los niños estén cansados.	It is possible that the children are tired.

... and after certain fixed expressions such as:

para que	in order that
para que llegue a tiempo	in order that he arrives on time
aunque	even if
aunque salga a las 6h00	even if he leaves at 6 o'clock
antes de que	before
antes de que compre su billete	before he buys his ticket
hasta que	until
hasta que llegue a la estación	until he arrives at the station

If in doubt, look in a good dictionary. There you will often find examples of expressions using these and other constructions, from which you can see when the subjunctive is necessary.

1.6.1 How to form the subjunctive

Put simply, the subjunctive is formed by swapping the endings of **-ar** verbs and **-er/-ir** verbs, using the **yo** form of the present tense, without **-o**, as the stem. So, for **-ar** verbs the subjunctive endings are: **-e**, **-es**, **-e**, **-emos**, **-éis**, **-en**, and for **-er** and **-ir** verbs the subjunctive endings are: **-a**, **-as**, **-a**, **-amos**, **-áis**, **-an**.

You will recognise most of these forms from the imperative use of the subjunctive (see 1.3.3 C and D). As you can see, the **yo** form does not end in **-o** as in the normal present tense (indicative), but is the same as the third person singular.

Fortunately, the endings are all familiar, and an easy way of recognising the subjunctive is when a verb seems to have an ending from 'the wrong set'! The same would apply if you needed to use the subjunctive yourself. Once you know one form, the others follow very predictably and easily.

Although there are irregular verbs, you will recognise them easily from their use as imperatives, and many are very common in everyday use.

A Regular verbs

yo form	hablar	yo form	comer	yo form	subir
hablo	hable	como	coma	subo	suba
	hables		comas		subas
	hable		coma		suba
	hablemos		comamos		subamos
	habléis		comáis		subáis
	hablen		coman		suban

B Stem-changing verbs

Stem-changing verbs are easy, because the stems change in the same places as in the present indicative. Here are some examples:

e→ie/-ar	e→ie/-er	e→ie/-ir	e→i	o→ue	o→ue	o→ue	u→ue
cerrar	entender	preferir	pedir	contar	volver	dormir	jugar
cierre	entienda	prefiera	pida	cuente	vuelva	duerma	juegue
cierres	entiendas	prefieras	pidas	cuentes	vuelvas	duermas	juegues
cierre	entienda	prefiera	pida	cuente	vuelva	duerma	juegue
cerremos	entendamos	prefiramos	pidamos	contemos	volvamos	durmamos	juguemos
cerréis	entendáis	prefiráis	pidáis	contéis	volváis	durmáis	juguéis
cierren	entiendan	prefieran	pidan	cuenten	vuelvan	duerman	jueguen

C   Irregular verbs

The most useful irregular verbs are ones which should be familiar to you because you will commonly see and hear them as instructions in public places.

infinitive	present yo form	subjunctive
ir	voy	vaya
ser	soy	sea
coger	cojo	coja
conducir	conduzco	conduzca
sacar	saco	saque
decir	digo	diga
saber	sé	sepa
seguir	sigo	siga
hacer	hago	haga
oír	oigo	oiga
poner	pongo	ponga
salir	salgo	salga
tener	tengo	tenga
traer	traigo	traiga
venir	vengo	venga

1.6.2   Expressions which take the subjunctive

The following expressions are always followed by the subjunctive. Choose two to memorise to use as a pattern.

Expressions of necessity

Hace falta que me vaya.   I have to go.

Futurity and purpose

Tomaremos té cuando lleguemos   We'll have some tea when we get
   a casa.   home.

Le llamaré para que sepa   I'll call him so that he finds out
   las noticias.   the news.

Antes de que vengan los visitantes, tenemos que limpiar la cocina. — Before the visitors arrive, we must clean the kitchen.

Continúe hasta que llegue a un cruce. — Continue until you come to a crossroads.

Wishes, influence or preferences

Quiero que llegue a tiempo. — I want him to be on time.

Prefiere que yo vaya allí. — He prefers me to go (there).

Possibility

Es posible que pueda venir. — It is possible that he can come.

Es imposible que llegue tarde. — It is not possible for him to be late.

Doubt and disbelief

No creo que esté enfermo. — I don't believe that he is ill.

No pienso que venga ella. — I don't think she will come.

Emotion and judgement

Siento que haya sido herido. — I am sorry that he has been hurt.

Es una lástima que no puedas venir. — It's a pity that you can't come.

Conjunctions or connectives such as *aunque* – although, even if

Aunque esté usted enfermo, debe presentarse en el tribunal. — Although you are ill, you have to go to court.

> Essentially, the subjunctive is used whenever the statement is looking forward, or refers to an unfulfilled or hypothetical action. Ask yourself 'did it happen/is it happening/will it happen?' If the answer is 'no', or 'not yet', you probably need the subjunctive.

Remember: The subjunctive forms for **usted** and **ustedes** are used as imperative forms, and those for **tú** and **vosotros/as** are used for negative commands.

1.6.3 Recognising the subjunctive

Even if you do not feel ready to use the subjunctive yet, it is useful to be able to recognise it when you hear it.

I Which verb is being used? Read the sentence and work out the infinitive of the word in italics.

a Es necesario que *venga*.　　He must come.

b No creo que *coja* el autobús.　　I don't believe he'll come by bus.

c Me alegra que *haga* buen　　I'm pleased that it's fine today.
tiempo hoy.

d ¡Espero que os *sintáis*　　I hope you feel welcome!
bienvenidos!

e Es posible que *estén* enfermos.　　It's possible that they are ill.

f Aunque *tenga* coche, siempre　　Even if she has a car, she will
irá a pie.　　always go on foot.

g Hace falta que lo *sepa* ella.　　She will have to know.

h Es imposible que se *pueda*　　It's impossible for it to be
terminar a tiempo.　　completed in time.

i Dudo que *tengan* un　　I don't think (I doubt) they have
coche nuevo.　　a new car.

j Siento mucho que *queráis* partir.　　I am sorry that you want to go.

1.6.4 ▶Fast track: The subjunctive

The subjunctive is used after certain verbs and expressions.

- It usually conveys a feeling of negativity, uncertainty, doubt or indecision: *I don't want (that) ..., I am not sure that ..., it is possible that ...*, etc.
- It is usually preceded by a conjunction or connective or another verb and **que** – *that. I hope/wish/doubt that ...*
- This means that it is usually the second verb in the sentence.

The subjunctive of most verbs is made from the stem of the **yo** form of the present tense. Remove the **-o** and then add these endings: for **-ar** verbs **-e, -es, -e, -emos, -éis, -en**, and for **-er** and **-ir** verbs **-a, -as, -a, -amos, -áis, -an**.

Although many of the most commonly-used verbs are irregular, some of their subjunctive forms are familiar as imperative forms in public notices and instructions.

You don't need to learn them, but it is useful to be able to recognise which verb they come from:

ir	vaya
ser	sea
coger	coja
conducir	conduzca
sacar	saque
saber	sepa
seguir	siga
oír	oiga
decir	diga
hacer	haga

poner	ponga
salir	salga
tener	tenga
traer	traiga
venir	venga

You can try to avoid using the subjunctive by:

- being positive and avoiding making negative statements!
- using **en mi opinión** or **a mi juicio** to express an opinion;
- using the infinitive instead of **que** + subjunctive where possible: **Hace falta que bebamos 2 litros de agua al día** (*We have to drink 2 litres of water a day*) becomes **Es necesario beber 2 litros de agua al día**.
- thinking of an easier way of saying it in English. Don't use two verbs joined by *that* in one sentence. Split it up and make two sentences: *I am sorry that he is ill* **(Siento que esté enfermo)** becomes **¿Está enfermo? ¡Lo siento!**

Choose two or three examples to memorise and use them as a pattern.

Just when you think you have learnt all the tenses, you pick up a book or a newspaper and find that there are even more. Fortunately, you don't have to learn to use them to speak good Spanish. If you want to know more about these other tenses, go to *¡Acción Gramática!* or *¡Viva la Gramática!* (P. Turk and M. Zollo).

1.7 ▶Fast track: Verbs

▶▶ **If you know when to use the different tenses, go on to 1.8.**

A Present tense

You use the present tense to talk about what is happening now ...

Leo.	I am reading.

... and to express generalisations:

No veo muchos programas de televisión.	I don't watch many television programmes.

These are the question forms:

¿Lees (tú) un periódico?	Do you read a daily paper?
¿Ves (tú) ...?	Do you watch ...?

B Perfect tense

You use the perfect tense to talk about what has happened in the very recent past.

He jugado al tenis.	I (have) played tennis.
He intentado.	I (have) tried.

These are the question forms:

¿Has jugado (tú)?	Have you played?
¿Has intentado (tú)?	Did you try?

C Imperfect tense

You use the imperfect tense to talk about what happened in the past if:

- it was a habitual action:

Jugaba cuando era pequeño/a.	I used to play when I was young.

- it was an ongoing and interrupted action:

Veía la televisión cuando oí a los vecinos gritar.	I was watching television when I heard the neighbours shout.

These are the question forms:

¿Jugabas (tú) ...?	Did you use to play ...?
¿Veías la televisión cuando ...?	Were you watching television when ...?

D Preterite tense

You use the preterite tense to talk about what has happened and finished in the past.

Jugué al tenis.	I played tennis.
Intenté.	I tried.

These are the question forms:

¿Jugaste (tú)?	Did you play?
¿Intentaste (tú)?	Did you try?

E Future immediate tense

You use the near future or future immediate to say what you are about to do.

Voy a ir.	I am going to go.
Va a partir.	He is going to leave.

These are the question forms:

¿Vas a ir?	Are you going to go?
¿Va a partir?	Is he going to leave?

F   Future simple tense
The future simple tense is used to express intention or say what you will do in the future.

Arreglaré mi despacho la semana que viene.	I will tidy my office next week.
Pronto iremos a México.	Soon we will go to Mexico.

These are the question forms:

¿Qué harás (tú)?	What will you do?
¿Cuándo partirás?	When will you go?

G   Imperative
The imperative is used to give orders or instructions.

¡Ve a buscar mis zapatillas!	Fetch me my slippers! (tú)
¡Cierre la puerta, por favor!	Shut the door, please! (usted)
Venid a verme pronto.	Come to see me soon. (vosotros)
Pongan sus maletas allí.	Put your suitcases there. (ustedes)

H   Interrogative
The interrogative is used to ask questions.

¿Tienes ...?	Have you got a ...?
¿Has visto ...?	Did you see ...?
¿Quiere usted entrar?	Do you want to come in?
¿Qué desea?	What would you like?

I   Conditional
The conditional is used to put things politely ...

Me gustaría ...	I would like ...
¿Podría usted ayudarme?	Could you help me?

... or to express conditions:

Yo te compraría un regalo si tuviera bastante dinero.	I would buy you a present if I had enough money.

J   Subjunctive
The subjunctive is used after certain verbs and expressions. It is usually preceded by another verb and **que**, meaning *that*. You can avoid having to use it yourself by keeping sentences simple.

Subjunctive verbs seem to have the 'wrong' endings: based on **-e** for **-ar** verbs, and based on **-a** for **-er** and **-ir** verbs.

Irregular subjunctives mostly sound familiar because they are often used for public notices and instructions. In any case, you should be able to tell which verb they come from:

sea – ser	vaya – ir	ponga – poner
tenga – tener	haga – hacer	sepa – saber

Recognising a verb

If a word that you don't know comes after a noun, the name of a person or a pronoun (**yo, tú, él, ella, usted, nosotros/as, vosotros/as, ellos, ellas** or **ustedes**), it is probably a verb.

■ If it ends in **-ar, -er, -ir, -arse, -erse** or **-irse**, it is an infinitive.

■ if it comes after a part of **haber** and ends in **-do**, it is a past participle of a verb.

■ If it ends in **-o, -as, -a, -amos, -áis, -an,** or **-o, -es, -e, -emos, -éis, -en,** or **-o, -es, -e, -imos, -ís, -en,** it is probably a verb in the present tense.

■ If it ends in **-aba, -abas, -ábamos, -abais, -aban** it is definitely an **ar** verb in the imperfect tense.

■ If it ends in **-ré, -rás, -rá, -remos, -réis, -rán,** it is definitely a verb in the future tense.

■ If it ends in **-ría, -rías, -ría, -ríamos, -ríais, -rían,** it is definitely a verb in the conditional tense.

■ if it ends in **-aste, -ó, -asteis, -aron,** or **-í, -iste, -ió, -isteis, -ieron** or **-eron**, it is a preterite form of a verb.

1.8 Useful expressions using verbs

▶▶ **If you know all these, go on to 1.8.11 Fast track**

1.8.1 To be or not to be: *ser* or *estar?*

A major issue in Spanish is choosing between the two verbs meaning *to be*. The easiest way to decide is to remember:

ser comes from Latin *esse – to be*, so use **ser** for what is of the *essence*, *essential*, i.e. to say what something or somebody *is* or is *like*.

I am a teacher, I am English, I am old.	Soy profesor, soy inglés, soy viejo.

estar comes from Latin *stare – to stand*, so use **estar** for position, *sta*tus and *sta*te resulting from an action, therefore for saying *where* something or somebody is, what their *status* is, or what *state* they are in.

I am at home, I am married, I am tired.	Estoy en casa, estoy casado, estoy cansado.

1.8.2 Special uses of *tener*

---

tener

---

tengo	tenemos
tienes	tenéis
tiene	tienen

Tener (*to have*) is used in many expressions, often where we would use the verb *to be* in English. Here are some examples.

A Expressing age
tener XX años – *to be XX years old*

¿Cuántos años tienes?	How old are you?
Tengo 21 años.	I am 21.

B Expressing heat and cold
tener calor/frío – *to be hot/cold*

Tengo frío.	I am cold.
¿Tiene usted frío?	Are you cold?
Tienen mucho frío.	They are very cold.
¿Tienes calor?	Are you hot?
Tenéis calor, ¿verdad?	You are hot, aren't you?

C Expressing hunger and thirst
tener hambre/sed – *to be hungry/thirsty*

Tengo hambre.	I am hungry.
¿Tienes sed?	Are you thirsty?
Ella tiene mucha sed.	She is very thirsty.
¿Tiene usted hambre?	Are you hungry?
No tenemos hambre.	We are not hungry.
¡Tenéis poca sed!	You are not very thirsty!

D Expressing fear
tener miedo de – *to be afraid of*

¡Tengo miedo de ti!	I am afraid of you!
Tenemos miedo del relámpago.	We are afraid of the lightning.
Ellos no tienen miedo de nada.	They fear nothing.

E Being right or wrong
tener razón – *to be right*

¡Tienes razón!	You are right!
Tengo razón, ¡a que sí!	I bet I am right!
No tenéis razón.	You are not right/You are wrong.

F Being in a hurry
tener prisa – *to be in a hurry*

Tengo prisa.	I am in a hurry.
¿Tienen ustedes mucha prisa?	Are you in much of a hurry?

G Being tired
tener sueño – *to be tired*

Tengo mucho sueño.	I am very tired.
¿Tienen ustedes sueño?	Are you tired?

H Being lucky or unlucky
tener suerte – *to be lucky*

¡Tienes suerte!	You are lucky!
Tenemos mucha suerte, ¿verdad?	We are very lucky, aren't we?
No tienen suerte.	They are not lucky.
Tiene mala suerte.	He is unlucky.

I Feeling like doing something
tener ganas de (+ infinitive) – *to feel like*

¿Tienes ganas de comer ahora?	Do you feel like eating now?
Tenía ganas de reir.	I felt like laughing.

J Having to do something
tener que (+ infinitive) – *to have to, must*

Tengo que salir.	I must go out.
¿Tienen que hablar con el director?	Do they have to talk to the principal?
Mi madre tuvo que ir al hospital ayer.	My mother had to go to hospital yesterday.

K Being painful
tener dolor de – *to have a pain in the .../to have a bad/sore ...*

Tengo dolor de cabeza.	I have a headache.
Tengo dolor de oídos.	I have an earache.
Ayer tuve dolor de pies.	Yesterday my feet ached.

NB: You can also say **me duele(n)**:

me duele el pie – my foot hurts; me duelen los pies – my feet hurt

Parts of the body which might hurt:

singular	plural	meaning
la cabeza		head
el ojo	los ojos	eye(s)
el oído	los oídos	ear(s) (inner)
la oreja	las orejas	ear(s) (outer)
el diente	los dientes	tooth, teeth (front)
la muela	las muelas	tooth, teeth (molars)
la mano	las manos	hand(s)
el dedo	los dedos	finger(s)
el brazo	los brazos	arm(s)
la pierna	las piernas	leg(s)
la rodilla	las rodillas	knee(s)
el pie	los pies	foot, feet
la espalda		back

I How would you say the following?

a I have a headache.
b Have you got a toothache? (tú)
c Her foot hurts.
d My arms ache.
e His knee hurts.
f Have you got a headache? (usted)
g She has earache.
h Do your eyes hurt? (vosotros)
i Does your back hurt? (ustedes)
j He has backache.

Checklist

These expressions take **tener** in Spanish:

tener ... años	to be ... years old
tener calor/frío	to be hot/cold
tener hambre/sed	to be hungry/thristy
tener miedo de	to be afraid of
tener razón	to be right/wrong
tener prisa	to be in a hurry
tener sueño	to be tired
tener suerte	to be lucky
tener ganas de ...	to feel like ...
tener que ...	to have to ...
tener dolor de ...	to have a pain in the ...

II How would you say the following?

a We are right.
b You are wrong. (tú)
c I am hot.

d He is thirsty.
e They are hungry.
f We are cold.
g I am thirsty.
h You are very tired. (usted)
i We arew lucky.
j I am in a hurry.

and some more:

k They are wrong.
l I am very cold.
m They are hot.
n We are thirsty.
o I am afraid of spiders.
p Are you thirsty? (tú)
q Are you cold? (usted)
r Do you feel like eating? (vosotros)
s Are you hungry? (ustedes)
t Are you right? (tú)
u You are wrong! (usted)
v Are you afraid? (vosotros)
w I am not afraid.
x He is not afraid.
y We have to go.
z He is always right.

1.8.3 There is/There are: *hay*

In Spanish, you say *(there) has* instead of *there is/are*. Note that the Spanish does not change for plural, but being an 'odd' part of **haber**, it can be used in other tenses:

Hay mucho que hacer.	There is a lot to do.
¿Hay fruta?	Is there any fruit?
Hay una pera …	There is one pear …
… y hay muchas naranjas.	… and there are lots of oranges.
No había pan.	There was no bread.
Había varios pasteles.	There were several cakes.
¿Habrá algo más?	Will there be anything else?
Sí, habrá unos bizcochos.	Yes, there will be some biscuits.
Ha habido un accidente.	There has been an accident.
Ayer hubo una tormenta.	Yesterday there was a storm.

I Now you try it.

a No ____ banco, pero ____ un cajero automático.

There isn't a bank but there is a cash machine.

b ____ muchas cajas en el supermercado, pero no ____ muchos cajeros …

There are lots of checkouts at the supermarket but there aren't many cashiers …

c ... pero afortunadamente, esta mañana no ____ colas.

... but luckily today there wasn't a queue.

d Antes ____ un autobús escolar, pero ahora no; no ____ suficientes niños ...

Before, there used to be a school bus, but not now; there aren't enough children ...

e ... esta mañana sólo ____ tres niños esperando un taxi.

... this morning there were only three children waiting for a taxi.

1.8.4 To know: *conocer* or *saber*?

There are two verbs meaning *to know* in Spanish – to know a fact: **saber** and to know a person or thing: **conocer**.

Saber is to know how to do something (as a result of learning how to do it).

sé, sabes, sabe, sabemos, sabéis, saben

Sé que Ana está casada. — I know Ana is married.

Sé conducir. — I know how to drive a car.

Sabía cocinar. — I used to know how to cook.

Conocer is to know a person, thing or place (to recognise by seeing, hearing, tasting or touching):

conozco, conoces, conoce, conocemos, conocéis, conocen

Le conozco muy bien. — I know him very well.

Mi amigo no conocía Madrid. — My friend didn't know Madrid.

I Which verb are you going to use? Use the appropriate part of the present tense.

a Yo ____ al señor Palomares desde hace mucho tiempo.
b Su hijo ____ a mi hijo.
c Nuestros niños ____ enviar correo electrónico.
d Nosotros ____ a la familia.
e Mi mujer ____ a su mujer.
f Mis padres ____ a sus padres.
g Ellos ____ bien la región donde viven.
h Mi mujer y yo, no ____ enviar e-mails.
i Mis padres no ____ utilizar un móvil.
j Mi hija ____ enviar fotos con su móvil.
k Yo no ____ enviar fotos por e-mail.

1.8.5 Impersonal verbs

Some Spanish verbs are used impersonally. These include the 'back-to-front verbs' **gustar**, **encantar** and others (see 1.2.2 G), which are used with the thing liked, loved, etc. as the subject:

I like coffee. — Me gusta el café.

I love Spanish wines. — Me encantan los vinos españoles.

1.8.6 To take, bring, look for, fetch, meet a person

These English verbs can be translated in various ways.

- **coger/tomar** – *to take transport*

  Cojo/Tomo el autobús.　　　　I am taking the bus.

- **llevar** – *to carry, take away (something you can carry)* (also: *to wear*)

  una pizza para llevar　　　　a take-away pizza

  – *to take (someone somewhere)*

  Llevé a mi tía al aeropuerto.　　I took my aunt to the airport.

- **buscar** – *to look for (something or someone); to fetch (someone)*

  Iré a buscarte a las diez.　　　I'll come and fetch/meet you at 10 o'clock.

- **traer** – *to bring (something you can carry, or someone)*

  Te he traído un pastel.　　　　I have brought you a cake.
  Trae a un amigo a la fiesta　　Bring a friend to the party
  　esta tarde si quieres.　　　　tonight, if you like.

This phrase will help you remember *to take away:*

1.8.7 To remember

- **recordar** – *to remember, to recall*

  This verb holds no surprises, but the following verb can also be used when more of an 'effort to remember' is implied, especially for remembering people.

- **acordarse de** – *to remember* (literally: *to remind yourself of*) (*something or someone*)

  In Spanish, you remind yourself *of* something:

  Me acuerdo de Marcos.　　　　I remember Marcos.
  Él no se acuerda de mí.　　　　He doesn't remember me.

Nos acordamos del día en que él llegó por primera vez.	We remember the day when he came for the first time.
Siempre recordaré el momento en que sufrí mi accidente.	I'll always remember the moment when I had the accident.
Lo recuerdo.	I remember it.
Mis padres no lo recuerdan.	My parents don't remember it.

I How would you say the following?

a I remember John.
b He remembers me.
c He remembers my house.
d We both remember the holidays.
e I remember his wife.
f I remember her smile.
g My children remember her.

NB: All of these could be expressed using either **recordar** or **acordarse de**.

 The opposite of **recordar** and **acordarse de** is **olvidar** – *to forget*; it is very easy to use, being a regular **-ar** verb.

1.8.8 Negative expressions

Negative statements include saying what you don't do, and expressions with *no, nothing, never, nobody*, etc.

How to say you don't do something

You already know to put **no** in front of the verb to express *not*.

No sé.	I don't know.
No hablo español.	I don't speak Spanish.
No como carne.	I don't eat meat.
Él no bebe vino.	He doesn't drink wine.
No viven en Madrid.	They don't live in Madrid.
¿Usted no está casado/a?	You aren't married?

Other negative expressions

These are all 'double negatives', where **no** goes in front of the verb and the other negative word after the verb.

no ... nunca/jamás – *never* (**nunca** is the more common)

Ella no ha ido nunca a Tenerife.	She has never been to Tenerife.
Nunca ha ido a Tenerife.	

 If you start with the negative word you don't need the marker **no**:
Nunca he ido – *I have never been.*

No … nada – *nothing/not anything*

No hice nada.   I didn't do anything.

no … nadie –   *nobody/no one*

No vio a nadie.   He didn't see anyone.

NB: Note the use of the personal **a** even in front of *nobody*!

no … ninguno(ningún)/a/os/as – *no*

No tengo ningún amigo.   I have no friends.

no … ni … ni – *not … either … or/neither … nor*

No tengo ni tiempo ni dinero.   I have neither time nor money.

> The idea of *any* in *not any* is not translated: **No tengo dinero** –
> *I haven't any money.*

I   How would you say the following? If possible, say them
    aloud so that you can get used to the sound of them. Then
    cover up the English, read them again and think about the
    meaning. Finally cover up the Spanish and translate the
    whole sentence.

a I have never been to Spain.   Yo ____ fui ____ a España.
b They didn't hurt anyone.   Ellos ____ hicieron daño a ____ .
c I never see Alicia.   ____ veo [____] a Alicia.
d They have nothing in their   ____ tienen ____ en su casa.
    house.
e You have never learned to   ¿____ aprendiste ____ a nadar?
    swim?
f I don't see anybody.   Yo ____ veo a ____ .
g She never rides a bike.   Ella ____ monta ____ en bicicleta.
h I have nothing in my pocket.   ____ tengo ____ en mi bolsillo.
i I have never been to Mallorca. ____ he ido a Mallorca.
j Nobody is at home.   ____ está en casa.

II   Match up these sentences.

a We haven't anything to eat.   **i**   No he tenido tiempo para ir
                                                al pueblo.
b Nobody has been shopping.   **ii** No hay ni pan ni queso.
c I didn't have time to go to town. **iii** No tengo dinero.
d There isn't any bread or cheese.   **iv** No tenemos nada para
                                                comer.
e You never go to the supermarket.   **v**   No vas nunca al
                                                supermercado.
f I haven't any money.   **vi** Nadie ha ido de compras.

> Remember, there is no need for *any* after a negative in Spanish.

¿Cómo?	How?
¿Dónde?	Where?
¿Adónde?	Where to?
¿Cuándo?	When?
¿Por qué?	Why?
¿Cuánto/a/os/as?	How much/many?
¿Cuánto tiempo?	How long?
¿Qué?	What?
¿Quién?	Who?
¿A quién?	Whom?

After these question words the verb follows, and you invert the order of the subject and the verb if a separate subject is expressed. (See 1.3.2.)

¿Adónde vais?	Where are you going?
¿Cómo va a Granada?	How is he going to Granada?
¿Por qué está en Almería?	Why is she in Almería?
¿Cuándo salís?	When are you leaving?
¿Qué hacéis vosotros?	What are you doing?
¿A quién conocen ustedes?	Who do you know?
¿Cuántos dormitorios tienes tú?	How many bedrooms do you have?
¿Qué vas a hacer?	What are you going to do?

I Which question word would you use?

a ¿_____ vive el señor Vicente?
b ¿_____ se llama su mujer?
c ¿_____ sale para Londres?
d ¿_____ va a Londres?
e ¿_____ va a hacer en Londres?
f ¿_____ tiene una cita en el banco?
g ¿_____ días se va a quedar en Londres?
h ¿_____ conoce en Londres?

1.8.10 Since (*desde hace*); to have just (*acabar de*)
In these expressions, you use a different tense in Spanish from the one you would expect to use in English.

A *Desde hace* – since
In English, when we want to say we have been doing something for a certain length of time, we use the past tense. In Spanish, because they have been doing it since (a year, etc.) and still are, they use the present tense.

Vivo aquí desde hace seis años.	I have lived here for six years.
Aprende el español desde hace dos años.	He has been learning Spanish for two years.

G Desde hace – since

You use **desde hace** to ask/answer the question *how long*:

¿Desde hace cuánto tiempo vives en Extremadura?	How long have you lived in Extremadura?
Vivo allí desde hace diez años.	I have lived there ten years. (lit: I live there since 10 years).

In Spanish, the verb is in the present tense because you still live there.

H Acabar de – to have just

Acabo de llegar.	I have just arrived. (literally: I am finishing arriving.)
Acaba de hacerlo.	He has just done it. (literally: He is finishing doing it.)

2 NOUNS AND DETERMINERS

How to recognise nouns

▶▶ **If you know what nouns and determiners are, go on to 2.1.**

Nouns are naming words. They tell you who somebody is (e.g. *he is a soldier, she is a mother*) or what something is (e.g. *it is a table, it is a rainbow*).

 You can recognise nouns because they can have words like *the, a* or *this* in front of them, e.g. *the* house, *a* dog, *this* car.

Sometimes the same word can be a noun or a verb.

the drink – to drink
the walk – to walk

I   There are ten nouns in this text. Can you find them all?

My sister has her own restaurant. She goes to the market each morning to buy fresh vegetables to make the soup for lunch. The other dishes she has prepared the night before and left ready to cook in the fridge.

A determiner is a word which comes in front of a noun to tell you (determine) which one it is: **the** *coat;* **a** *coat;* **my** *coat;* **your** *coat;* **this** *coat;* **which** *coat?*

2.1 Nouns and gender

▶▶ **If you know about the gender of nouns, go on to 2.2.**

In Spanish, all nouns are either masculine or feminine.

The word for *bottle* – **botella** – is a feminine word.
The word for *plate* – **plato** – is a masculine word.

Feminine words are usually indicated by *nf* in the dictionary
(*n* – noun *f* – feminine) and masculine words by *nm*.

2.2 Nouns and the words for 'the': *el* and *la*

The word *the* is a determiner. It is also called the definite
article because it refers to a definite thing, e.g. *the* house
you live in and not just any house.

▶▶ **If you know about el and la and the gender of
nouns, go on to 2.3.**

In Spanish, all nouns are either masculine or feminine.

- The word for *the* in front of a masculine noun is **el**.

  el niño   the boy
  el bolso   the bag

- The word for *the* in front of a feminine noun is **la**.

  la niña   the girl
  la puerta   the door

I   Put the correct form (**el** or **la**) in front of these.

  a _____ coche (m)   car
  b _____ aceituna (f)   olive
  c _____ bocadillo (m)   sandwich
  d _____ bolígrafo (m)   ballpoint pen, biro
  e _____ ciudad (f)   town, city
  f _____ pez (m)   fish
  g _____ acera (f)   pavement
  h _____ autopista (f)   motorway
  i _____ ferrocarril (m)   railway
  j _____ deporte (m)   sport
  k _____ billete (m)   ticket

II Now do the same for these places.

  a _____ casa (f)   house
  b _____ gasolinera (f)   petrol station
  c _____ estación (f)   station
  d _____ calle (f)   street
  e _____ avenida (f)   avenue
  f _____ garaje (m)   garage
  g _____ tienda (f)   shop
  h _____ banco (m)   bank
  i _____ oficina de correos (f) post office
  j _____ puente (m)   bridge

When a feminine noun begins with a stressed **ha** or **a** you
have to use **el** instead of **la**.

el agua	the water
el hambre	the hunger

III Fill in the gaps with **el** or **la**.

a	_____ aceite (m)	oil
b	_____ helado (m)	ice-cream
c	_____ abrigo (m)	coat
d	_____ baño (m)	bath
e	_____ ensalada (f)	salad
f	_____ oficina (f)	office
g	_____ burro (m)	donkey
h	_____ médico (m)	doctor
i	_____ agenda (f)	diary
j	_____ entrada (f)	entrance
k	_____ desayuno (m)	breakfast
l	_____ viaje (m)	journey
m	_____ agua (f)	water
n	_____ zumo (m)	juice
o	_____ hombre (m)	man
p	_____ carta (f)	letter, menu
q	_____ escuela (f)	school
r	_____ mano (f)	hand
s	_____ ventana (f)	window
t	_____ pollo (m)	chicken

2.2.1 The neutral article: *lo*

Abstract and general nouns can be made by using the indeterminate form **lo** and the masculine form of the adjective (although this can refer to both genders).

lo inesperado	the unexpected
lo contrario	the opposite
lo bueno	the good

2.3 Nouns and the words for 'the' in the plural: *los* and *las*

▶▶ **If you know about the plural, go on to 2.4.**

In the plural, the word for *the* with all feminine words is **las** and the word for *the* with all masculine nouns is **los**.

singular	plural
el gato	los gatos
la casa	las casas

To make the plural of the noun in English, we usually add an **-s**. In Spanish, most words make their plural by adding **-s** unless they end in a consonant, in which case they add **-es**.

la piscina → las piscinas; el perro → los perros; la catedral → las catedrales

Some singular masculine nouns are non-gender-specific in the plural.

el hermano – the brother → los hermanos – the siblings, brothers and sisters

2.3.1 Common irregular plurals

The following categories of nouns form their plurals in different ways.

- Nouns ending in **-z** form their plural by changing the **z** to **c** and adding **-es**.
  el pez – the fish → los peces – the fish(es)

- Some nouns lose or gain an accent in the plural.
  el inglés – the Englishman → los ingleses – the English people
  el joven – the young man → los jóvenes – the young people

- Nouns which end in **-s** and have an unstressed last syllable don't change in the plural.
  la crisis – the crisis → las crisis – the crises

I   Put these words into the plural.

a el pez   the fish
b el gato   the cat
c el barco   the boat
d la terraza   the terrace
e el padre   the parent
f la mosca   the fly
g el castillo   the castle
h el alemán   the German
i el español   the Spaniard

2.4 Nouns and the words for 'a': *un* and *una*

The word *a* is a determiner. It is also called the indefinite article because it refers to any *one* item and not a specific one, e.g. *a* bottle of red wine, not *the* bottle that you have chosen specifically.

▶▶ **If you know all about un and una, go on to 2.5.**

- The word for *a* in front of a masculine noun is **un**.
  un vaso   a glass

- The word for *a* in front of a feminine noun is **una**.

  una taza   a cup

I   Imagine you are talking about your family. How would you say you have one of all these?

Tengo ...

a ____ hermano   **f** ____ tía
b ____ hermana   **g** ____ suegro
c ____ abuelo   **h** ____ prima
d ____ abuela   **i** ____ suegra
e ____ tío   **j** ____ perro

2.4.1   Nouns with masculine and feminine forms

Some nouns have a masculine and a feminine form. The masculine form usually ends in **-o**, and to form the feminine form you usually replace the **-o** with an **-a**, or add an **-a** if it ends in a consonant. If the word ends in **-e** there is no change, and for nouns ending in **-ista** there is no change either.

un amigo → una amiga   a friend
un empleado → una empleada   an employee
un vecino → una vecina   a neighbour
un bailador → una bailadora   a dancer
un estudiante → una estudiante   a student
un cantante → una cantante   a singer
un automovilista → una automovilista   a car driver

BUT

un actor → una actriz   an actor/an actress

In Spanish, you omit the indefinite article when stating people's occupations, religions, nationality, etc.

Soy estudiante.   I am a student.
Es americano.   He is American.
Juan es médico.   Juan is a doctor.
¿Eres católico?   Are you a Catholic?

I   How would you say the following?

     a Juan is a dancer.
     b Rodríguez is a student.
     c Ramón is a singer.
     d Enrique is an actor.
     e Estrellita is a Catholic.
     f Pilar is an employee.
     g She is a car driver.

To talk about more than one thing in English we say *some* or *any*. Usually this word is just omitted in Spanish. The plural forms of **un** and **una** (**unos** and **unas**) can be used to mean *some*, but these are not generally expressed.

Tengo apartamentos.	I have some flats.
Tengo casas.	I have some houses.

If you are saying you haven't any of something, you don't need a word for *any*:

No tengo apartamentos.	I haven't any flats.
No tengo casas.	I haven't any houses.

2.5 How to tell if a noun is masculine or feminine

It is not always possible to tell whether a word is masculine or feminine in Spanish. It is helpful to learn nouns along with their word for *the* (**el** or **la**). There are also some other ways of working out if a word is masculine of feminine:

- If you hear **el** or **un** being used in front of it, it is masculine.
- If you hear **la** or **una** being used in front of it, it is feminine.
- If you hear **los** or **unos** being used in front of it, it is masculine plural.
- If you hear **las** or **unas** being used in front of it, it is feminine plural.

In addition to this, there are some rules – but there are also a lot of exceptions! The following endings usually mean that a noun is masculine:

-o	el año	year
-e	el viaje	voyage/trip
-l	el metal	metal
-n	el atún	tuna
-r	el bar	bar
-s	el país	country

The following endings usually mean that a noun is feminine:

-a	la boca	mouth
-ad	la verdad	truth
-z	la vez	time/turn
-ción	la noción	notion/idea
-sión	la precisión	precision
-ud	la salud	health

However, because there are a lot of exceptions to these rules, you still can't be certain of a noun's gender unless you check it in the dictionary. When you look up a word in the dictionary, it usually tells you the gender of the word in brackets after it: **casa** (f) *house*; **pueblo** (m) *village*.

I Now put **el** or **la** in front of these words. The rules above will help you.

a ____ emoción
b ____ ensalada
c ____ jabón
d ____ mariposa
e ____ manifestación
f ____ hotel
g ____ ciudad
h ____ francés
i ____ esbeltez
j ____ cuervo
k ____ cicatriz
l ____ carrera
m ____ panadería
n ____ camisa
o ____ zapatero
p ____ mercado
q ____ luz
r ____ trabajo
s ____ autopista
t ____ nación

2.6 'My', 'your', 'his', 'her', etc.: possessive adjectives

▶▶ **If you know all about these words, go on to 2.7.**

These are words for saying what belongs to whom: *my coat*, *his umbrella*, *your briefcase*, *their house*, *our cat*, etc.

In English, we only have one form of each: *my, your, his, her, our, their.* In Spanish, there are singular and plural forms to agree with their nouns (but no masculine and feminine forms except in the case of **nuestro/a** and **vuestro/a**).

	singular	plural
my	mi	mis
your (fam. sing.)	tu	tus
his/her/its	su	sus
your (formal sing.)	su	sus

	masc	fem	masc	fem
our	nuestro	nuestra	nuestros	nuestras
your (fam. plural)	vuestro	vuestra	vuestros	vuestras
their	su		sus	
your (formal plural)	su		sus	

2.6.1 My (*mi, mis*)

The word for *my* agrees in number but not in gender with the person or thing it is describing. This means that you use the singular form (**mi**) with singular nouns of either gender:

mi hermano	my brother
mi madre	my mother
mi perro	my dog

My in front of plural nouns is **mis**, in both masculine and feminine:

| mis gatos | my cats |
| mis hermanas | my sisters |

I **Mi** or **mis**?

a _____ gatos
b _____ hermana
c _____ madre
d _____ padres
e _____ libros
f _____ casa
g _____ abuelos
h _____ tarjeta
i _____ peces
j _____ pluma

II   Now do the same for your clothes ...

a _____ pantalón
b _____ camisa
c _____ jersey
d _____ calcetines
e _____ zapatos
f _____ chaqueta
g _____ abrigo
h _____ bufanda
i _____ guantes
j _____ paraguas

III   ... and your family. Imagine you are showing someone photographs of your family. What would you say?

Es mi .../Son mis ...

a _____ niños
b _____ marido
c _____ mujer
d _____ padre
e _____ madre
f _____ hermana
g _____ hermanos
h _____ abuelos
i _____ primo
j _____ hijo
k _____ hijas

2.6.2   Your (tu, tus)

You can only use **tu** or **tus** (the familiar singular form) when speaking to a child or pet, or someone you know very well.

▶▶   **If you are not going to need this form (it behaves just like the mi/mis form), go on to 2.6.3.**

The words for *your* (**tu, tus**) are similar to the words for *my* (**mi, mis**) and behave in the same way.

I   Put **tu** or **tus** in front of these words.

Es tu .../Son tus ...

a _____ niños
b _____ padre
c _____ madre
d _____ hermanas
e _____ hermano
f _____ abuelos
g _____ hija
h _____ hijos
i _____ perros
j _____ gato

II How would you ask what they are called?

¿Cómo se llama tu ...?/¿Cómo se llaman tus ...?

a _____ colegas
b _____ colega
c _____ amigo
d _____ amigas
e _____ amigos
f _____ amiga
g _____ hermano
h _____ hermanas
i _____ abuelos
j _____ padres

2.6.3 His, her and its (su, sus)

The words for *his/her* (**su, sus**) rhyme with **tu** and **tus** and are used in the same way.

Notice that:
* **su hermano** means both *his brother* and *her brother*;
* **su hermana** means both *his sister* and *her sister;*
* **sus amigos** means both *his friends* and *her friends.*

These words are also used for *your* when you are using the formal **usted** and **ustedes** forms of address (see 2.6.7)

▶▶ **If you know all about su and sus, go on to 2.6.4.**

I Talk about Tomás by filling in the right word (**su, sus**).

a _____ amigas se llaman Pilar y María.
b _____ primo se llama José.
c _____ hermano es grande.
d _____ madre es escultora.
e _____ padre trabaja en el Banco de España.
f _____ hermanas son profesoras.
g _____ hermano menor tiene sólo ocho años.
h _____ deporte favorito es el tenis.
i _____ comidas favoritas son la pizza 'Cuatro estaciones' y los espaguetis.
j _____ color favorito es el azul oscuro.

> In sentences like these, you can't tell the gender of a noun by the (determiner) word in front of it, but if there is an adjective attached, this will usually tell you all you need to know!

II Now do the same for Alegría's family and friends.

a _____ amiga se llama Conchita.
b _____ novio se llama Esteban.
c _____ hermanos se llaman Javier y Ramón.
d _____ hermana se llama Consuelo.
e ¿Cómo se llaman _____ padres?
f _____ monopatín es negro y amarillo.
g _____ pasatiempo favorito es el patinaje.
h _____ colores favoritos son el rojo y el blanco.
i _____ comida favorita es la paella.
j _____ bebidas favoritas son la sangría y la leche.

2.6.4 Our (nuestro/a, nuestros/as)

▶▶ **If you know all about nuestro/a and vuestro/a, go on to 2.6.6.**

The words for *our* are **nuestro**/**nuestros** and **nuestra**/**nuestras**. Unlike the other possessive adjectives you have met so far, they change for the singular and plural *and* the masculine and feminine: **nuestro apartamento, nuestra casa, nuestros coches, nuestras tiendas**.

I How would you say these are *our* things?

Es nuestro/a ..../Son nuestros/as ...

a _____ casa
b _____ apartamento
c _____ perros
d _____ bodega
e _____ vinos
f _____ garaje
g _____ coche
h _____ jardín
i _____ árbol
j _____ dormitorios

2.6.5 Your (vuestro/a, vuestros/as)

The word for *your* (familiar plural form) is easy to remember because it rhymes with **nuestro/a** and **nuestros/as** and behaves in the same way: **vuestro hijo, vuestras hermanas**.

I Ask if these are *your* things.

¿Es vuestro/a .../¿Son vuestros/as ...

a _____ oficina?
b _____ silla?
c _____ ordenador?

d _____ libros?
e _____ abrigo?
f _____ guantes?
g _____ paraguas?
h _____ documentos?
i _____ cartera?
j _____ llaves?

2.6.6 Their (su, sus)

The words for *their* are **su** and **sus** – the same as the words for *his/her/its*. They rhyme with the words for *your* (**tu**, **tus**) and behave in the same way.

These words are also used to express *your* when you are using the formal **usted/ustedes** forms (see 2.6.7).

I Say these are *their* things.

Es su .../Son sus ...

a _____ coche
b _____ garaje
c _____ bicis
d _____ jardín
e _____ flores
f _____ plantas
g _____ casa
h _____ puerta
i _____ ventanas
j _____ balcón

2.6.7 Your (formal) (su, sus)

The words for *your* (formal **usted** and **ustedes** forms – for talking to strangers, people older than you, etc.) are the same in form as the words for *his/her/its* and *their* (**su/sus**), and work in the same way.

Deme su pasaporte, por favor.	Give me your passport, please.
Señora, ¿éstos son sus niños?	Madam, are these your children?
Caballeros, pueden aparcar su coche allí.	Gentlemen, you can park your car there.
Señoras y señores, ¡no dejen sus maletas allí, por favor!	Ladies and gentlemen, please don't leave your suitcases there!

I Ask if these are *your* things, using the formal form **su/sus**.

¿Es su ...?/¿Son sus ...?

a _____ gato
b _____ silla
c _____ libros

d _____ pies
e _____ jersey
f _____ tazas
g _____ hermanos
h _____ moto
i _____ cama
j _____ plumas

2.6.8 ▶Fast track: Nouns and Determiners

All nouns in Spanish are either masculine or feminine.

- The word for *the* with masculine singular nouns is **el**.
- The word for *the* with feminine singular nouns is **la**.

- The word for *the* with masculine plural nouns is **los**.
- The word for *the* with feminine plural nouns is **las**.

- The word for *a* with masculine nouns is **un**.
- The word for *a* with feminine nouns is **una**.

When saying what people *are* or *do* (their jobs, nationalities, etc.) you usually omit the *a* in Spanish:

Soy estudiante.   I am (a) student.

A does not have a plural of its own. The plural of 'a' in English would be 'some' or 'any', but it is usually omitted in Spanish:

Busco libros.   I am looking for (some) books.
No busco libros.   I am not looking for (any) books.

However, in Spanish, the plural forms **unos** and **unas** are sometimes used to indicate a number of items without being specific, rather like English *some*:

Necesito unos libros más   I need some more modern
  modernos.   books.
Tiene unas flores magníficas.   She has some magnificent
                                     flowers.

This plural form can also be used to indicate an approximate number, being equivalent to 'some' when it means 'about':

Mi abuelo tiene unos   My grandfather is about 80 years
  ochenta años.   old.
Lo visité hace unas tres   I visited him about three weeks
  semanas.   ago.

It is a good idea to learn Spanish nouns with *the* (**el** and **la**): **la comida**; **el gato**.

How to translate *my, your, his, her, its,* etc.:

	with singular nouns	with plural nouns
my	mi	mis
your (familiar singular)	tu	tus
his/her/its	su	sus
their	su	sus
your (formal sing. and pl.)	su	sus

Our and *your* (familiar plural) change according to number and gender:

	with masc. sing. nouns	with fem. sing. nouns	with masc. pl. nouns	with fem. pl. nouns
our	nuestro	nuestra	nuestros	nuestras
your (familiar plural)	vuestro	vuestra	vuestros	vuestras

2.7 More determiners

Remember, determiners are words which come before a noun and say 'which' one it is. You already know some but there are others.

Ones you already know: **the** *table,* **a** *table,* **my** *table,* **your** *table*

Some new ones: **which** *table?,* **all** *tables,* **the same** *table,* **several** *tables,* **some** *tables,* **every** *table.*

If you do not think you need these yet, leave them and come back to them later.

el/la, los/las	the
un/una, unos/unas	a/some
mi, mis	my
este/esta, estos/estas	this/these
¿cuánto/cuánta?, ¿cuántos/cuántas?	how much/how many?
otro/otra, otros/otras	(an)other
mucho/mucha, muchos/muchas	much/many
poco/poca, pocos/pocas	little (of)/few
tanto/tanta, tantos/tantas	so much/many
demasiado/demasiada, demasiados/demasiadas	too much/too many

todo/toda, todos/todas	all/every
ambos/ambas	both
cierto/cierta, ciertos/ciertas	(a) certain
mismo/misma, mismos/mismas	same
varios/as	several
algún/alguno/alguna, algunos/algunas	some/any/a few
ningún/ninguno/ninguna	no/not any/none/nobody

2.7.1 This, these: *este/esta* and *estos/estas*

The demonstrative adjectives **este/esta**, etc. are used to point to a particular thing or things: *this page, this book, these clothes.*

singular		plural	
masculine	**feminine**	**masculine**	**feminine**
este	esta	estos	estas

I   Put the correct form (**este/esta** or **estos/estas**) in front of these words.

a _____ hotel es muy bueno. — This hotel is very good.
b Detrás de _____ casa, hay un jardín. — Behind this house there is a garden.
c En _____ jardín crecen plantas. — In this garden, they grow plants.
d _____ personas trabajan en el jardín. — These people work in the garden.
e _____ flores son raras. — These flowers are rare.

2.7.2 That, those: *ese/esa/esos/esas* and *aquel/aquella/aquellos/aquellas*

Spanish has two demonstrative adjectives which translate the English *that/those.* **Ese/esa**, etc. is used to point to something further away than *this* but still quite close to you: *that book, those clothes (just there)*, and **aquel/aquella**, etc. to point to something still further away: *that car, those houses (over there).*

singular		plural	
masculine	**feminine**	**masculine**	**feminine**
ese	esa	esos	esas
aquel	aquella	aquellos	aquellas

I   Put the correct form **aquel/aquella/aquellos/aquellas** in front of these words.

a _____ árbol es muy viejo.   That tree is very old.
b _____ puerta está reservada   That door is reserved for
     para los visitantes.   visitors.
c _____ folletos son gratuitos.   Those brochures are free.
d _____ hombre saca fotos.   That man is taking photographs.
e En _____ jardín hay muchos   In that garden there are lots of
     narcisos.   daffodils.

2.7.3   ¿Cuánto/Cuánta? and ¿Cuántos/Cuántas?

¿Cuánto/Cuánta? and **¿Cuántos/Cuántas?** mean *how much* and *how many*, and agree in number and gender with the noun.

singular		plural	
masculine	**feminine**	**masculine**	**feminine**
¿cuánto?	¿cuánta?	¿cuántos?	¿cuántas?

I   Put in the correct form: **cuánto/cuánta/cuántos/cuántas.**

a ¿_____ dinero tienes?   How much money have you got?
b ¿_____ manzanas quieres?   How many apples do you want?
c ¿_____ tiempo pasaron allí?   How much time did they spend
                                         there?
d ¿_____ coches están en la calle? How many cars are in the street?

2.7.4   Some, other, all, any, every, etc.

These adjectives agree in the normal way with the noun (but note that some, such as **ambos** and **ambas**, are only used in the plural).

otro/otra, otros/otras ((an)other)

Deme otro bolígrafo.   Give me a different biro.
Tienes otra hija, ¿verdad?   You have another daughter,
                                  haven't you?
Tengo otros hijos que no   I have other sons who don't live
   viven aquí.   here.
Necesitamos otras seis personas. We need six more/other people.

mucho/mucha, muchos/muchas (much, many)

Tiene mucho trabajo.   He/She has a lot of work.
Tienen mucha basura.   They have a lot of rubbish.
¿Tienes muchos amigos?   Have you got lots of friends?
Mi amiga sacó muchas fotos.   My friend took lots of photos.

poco/poca, pocos/pocas (little, few)

Tenemos muy poco tiempo.	We have very little time.
Mi madre tiene poca paciencia.	My mother has little patience.
Mi hermano tiene pocos amigos.	My brother has few friends.
Habla con pocas palabras.	He speaks with few words.

tanto/tanta, tantos/tantas (so much, so many)

¡No me des tanto!	Don't give me so much!
¡Hay tanta gente!	There are so many people!
No tenemos tantos coches como ellos.	We haven't as many cars as they have.
Su amiga tiene tantas tías.	Her friend has so many aunts.

demasiado/a, demasiados/as (too much, too many)

Tengo demasiado trabajo.	I have too much work.
¡Había demasiada gente!	There were too many people!
Los vecinos tienen demasiados coches.	The neighbours have too many cars.
Saqué demasiadas fotos.	I took too many photos.

todo/toda, todos/todas (all, every)

todo el tiempo	all the time
toda la familia	all the family
todos los otros	all the others (masculine)
todas las otras	all the others (feminine)
todas las flores	all the flowers/every flower
todos los días	every day
todas las semanas	every week

ambos/ambas (both)

Ambos tienen un coche rojo.	They both have a red car.
Le di ambas partes del documento.	I gave him both parts of the document.

cierto/cierta, ciertos/ciertas ((a) certain)

Cierto chico salió con ella.	A certain boy went out with her.
Me dio cierta noticia ...	She gave me a certain piece of news ...
Ciertos coches son más rápidos.	Certain cars are faster.
Para ciertas personas no tiene importancia.	For certain people it's not important.

mismo/misma, mismos/mismas (same)

Es del mismo color.	It is the same colour.
Tenemos la misma amiga.	We have the same girlfriend.
Vamos a los mismos sitios.	We go to the same places.
Les gustan las mismas cosas.	They like the same things.

varios/varias

Varios/as means *several*. Obviously, it is always plural, but it agrees in gender with the noun it refers to.

Tuve que escuchar varios discos compactos.	I had to listen to several CDs.
¡Ya te lo conté varias veces!	I have already told you several times!

algún/alguno/alguna, algunos/algunas (some/any/a few)

Algún means *some, any*, etc. The form **algún** is used before masculine nouns, while **alguno** is used by itself, as a pronoun; **alguna** is used both before feminine nouns and by itself.

¿Tienes algún tiempo libre?	Have you got any free time?
Tengo algunos minutos.	I've got a few minutes.
Tengo algunos, pero no muchos.	I've got a few but not many.

ningún/ninguno/ninguna (no/not any/none/nobody)

Ningún is a negative word meaning *no, no one*, etc. It is used together with **no** (*not*), which reinforces it rather than cancelling it out as it would in English. The form **ningún** is used before masculine nouns, while **ninguno** is used by itself, as a pronoun; **ninguna** is used both before feminine nouns and by itself.

¿No tienes ningún amigo?	Haven't you got any friends?
No, no tengo ninguno.	No, I have none.
¡No hay ninguna botella de agua aquí!	There is no bottle of water here!

3 PRONOUNS

What is a pronoun?

A pronoun is a word which stands for a noun. Instead of saying:

- *Mr Jones*, you can say *he:* **él**
- *the woman*, you can say *she:* **ella**
- *my husband/wife and I*, you can say *we:* **nosotros/nosotras** (use **nosotros** for masculine nouns and a mixture of genders, and use **nosotras** for feminine nouns)
- *Señor y Señora Gómez*, you can say *they:* **ellos/ellas** (use **ellos** for masculine nouns and a mixture of genders, and use **ellas** for feminine nouns)

In English, instead of saying *table* we say *it*. In Spanish, everything is either masculine or feminine, so *the table* is *she* (**ella**) and *the book* is *he* (**él**).

But don't forget that in Spanish the subject pronouns are almost always left out, because the ending on the verb does their job and tells you who or what is the subject of the verb.

3.1 *yo, tú, usted, él, ella*, etc.: subject pronouns

▶▶ **If you know what a subject pronoun is, go on to 3.2.**

The subject is the person who or the thing which does the action: *I run, you play, he eats, she drinks, it shuts, we live, you swim, they talk.*

The subject pronouns in Spanish are as follows.

singular	plural
yo	nosotros/as
tú	vosotros/as
él	ellos
ella	ellas
usted	ustedes

3.1.1 *Yo – I:* the first person singular

You use the first person when you are talking about yourself. It translates *I.*

yo soy	I am
yo duermo	I am sleeping
yo bebo	I am drinking
yo escucho	I am listening
yo me llamo Peter y vivo ...	I am called Peter and I live ...

Yo is only written with a capital letter at the beginning of a sentence.

With **yo** the verb almost always ends in **-o** in the present tense; four verbs have **yo** endings in **-oy**.

3.1.2 *Tú – you:* the familiar singular form

You use **tú** when you are talking to one person you know very well, to someone who has invited you to do so, or to a child or pet. It translates *you.*

¿Tú tienes un perro?	Have you got a dog?
¿Has ido a Madrid?	Did you go to Madrid?

With **tú** the verb always ends in **-as**, **-ás** or **-es** in the present tense.

3.1.3 *Él/ella – he/she/it:* the third person singular

You use **él/ella** when you are talking about someone or something else. These words translate *he*, *she* and *it.*

Remember that in Spanish everything is either masculine or feminine. *A chair* is feminine, so if you want to say something about *it*, you have to use **ella** (*she*); similarly, *a book* is masculine so if you want to refer to *it*, you have to say **él** (*he*).

La vió ella.	She saw it.
Me vio él.	He saw me.

With **él/ella** the verb ends in **-a**, **-á** or **-e** in the present tense, except for *he/she/it is* – **es**.

3.1.4 *Usted – you:* the formal singular form

You use **usted** when you are talking to one person you don't know very well, your boss at work, your teacher, someone who is older than you, etc. It translates *you.*

Note that you use the third person of the verb with **usted**, so the verb ends in **-a**, **-á** or **-e** in the present tense, except for *you are* – **usted es**.

¿Usted es profesor?	Are you a teacher?
¿Es usted española?	Are you Spanish?
Usted habla español, ¿no?	You do speak Spanish, don't you?
Usted tiene una casa bonita.	You have. a pretty house.

3.1.5 *Nosotros/as* – we: the first person plural

You use **nosotros** to talk about yourself and one or more other people, when the people are all male or a mixture of males and females. Use **nosotras** when you are talking about yourself and one or more other people, all of whom are female. You use these words when you would use *we* in English.

After **nosotros/as** the verb always ends in **-amos, -emos** or **-imos** in the present tense, except for *we are* – **somos**.

Nosotros (Juan, María y yo) vamos al parque.	We are going to the park.
Nosotras (Paquita y yo – Josefa) fuimos a la playa.	We went to the beach.

3.1.6 *Vosotros/as* – you: the familiar plural form

You use **vosotros** when you are talking to two or more male people you know well, or who are younger than you, related to you, etc. You also use it for a mixture of male and female people you know or who are younger than you. Use **vosotras** for two or more female people you know well or who are younger than you. These words translate *you*.

With **vosotros/as** the verb always ends in **-áis, -éis** or **-ís** in the present tense, except for *you are* – **sois**.

Vosotros dos (Juan y Miguel), ¿qué pensáis?	What do you two think?
Vosotras (Marta y María), ¿estáis conmigo o no?	Are you two with me or not?

3.1.7 *Ellos/ellas* – they: the third person plural

You use **ellos/ellas** when you are talking about more than one person or thing. These words translate *they*.

You use **ellos** to refer to:

- more than one masculine person or thing;
- a mixture of masculine and feminine people or things.

You only use **ellas** if all the people or things are feminine.

After **ellos/ellas** the verb ends in **-an**, **-án** or **-en** in the present tense, except for *they are* – **son**.

Ellos viven al final de la calle.   They live at the end of the street.
Ellas (Virginia e Isabel) trabajan   They work in Madrid.
   en Madrid.

3.1.8 *Ustedes* – you: the formal plural form

You use **ustedes** when you are talking to two or more people of either gender whom you don't know, who are older than you, etc. It also translates *you*.

Note that you use the third person of the verb with **ustedes**, so the verb ends in **-an**, **-án** or **-en** in the present tense, except for *you are* – **son**.

Pasen ustedes por aquí, y siéntense.   Come this way and sit down.

I   Which subject pronoun should you use?

a I am going to the cinema tonight.
b After the cinema we are going to a restaurant.
c My girlfriends will be there.
d The boys are going to a football match.
e Lucas is playing.
f Isabel is going to watch.
g Where are you going?

II Add the correct subject pronoun to these sentences.

a Juan vive en España. ____ vive en el norte.
b Pablo y Mariana viven en el sur. ____ viven en Málaga.
c ¿Yo? ____ vivo en Madrid.
d ¿Dónde vive ____ , señor?
e Yo vivo en el centro de Madrid con mis amigos. ____ vivimos en un gran piso en la calle de Alcalá.
f Mari-Carmen y Sofía viven en el barrio norte. ____ tienen un pequeño apartamento.
g Mi hermana vive en León. ____ estudia en la universidad de León.
h Mis abuelos viven en la Alcarria. ____ tienen una granja.
i ¿Dónde vives ____ ?
j Mi hermano juega al tenis. ____ juega muy bien.

3.1.9 ▶Fast track: Subject pronouns

A pronoun is a word which stands for a noun: *I run, **you** play, **he** eats, **she** drinks, **it** shuts, **we** live, **you** swim, **they** talk.*

The subject is the person who or thing which does the action.

Subject pronouns are normally omitted in Spanish, but when you do use them (usually for emphasis or clarification), they are as follows:

You use **yo** (first person singular) when you are talking about yourself. After **yo** the verb usually ends in **-o** in the present tense.

You use **tú** (*you*, familiar singular form) when you are talking to one person you know very well, to someone who has invited you to do so, or to a child or pet. After **tú** the verb ends in **-as**, **-ás** or **-es** in the present tense.

You use **usted** (*you*, formal singular form) when you are talking to one person you don't know very well, someone who is older than you, etc. After **usted** the verb is in the third person form and ends in **-a**, **-á** or **-e** in the present tense.

You use **él/ella** (third person singular) to translate *he, she* and *it*. In Spanish, everything is either masculine or feminine, so *the table* (**la mesa**) is *she* (**ella**) and *the book* (**el libro**) is *he* (**él**). After **él/ella** the verb usually ends in **-a**, **-á** or **-e** in the present tense.

You use **nosotros/as** (first person plural) to talk about yourself and someone else (**nosotros** for two or more males or a mixture of males and females, and **nosotras** for all females). You use it when you would use *we* in English. After **nosotros/as** the verb ends in **-amos**, **-emos** or **-imos** in the present tense.

You use **vosotros/as** (familiar plural form) to translate *you* when talking to people you know quite well (**vosotros** for two or more males or a mixture of males and females, and **vosotras** for all females). After **vosotros/as** the verb usually ends in **-áis**, **-éis** or **-ís** in the present tense.

You use **ustedes** (*you*, formal plural form) when you are talking to two or more people of either gender whom you don't know, who are older than you, etc. After **ustedes** the verb is in the third person form and usually ends in **-an**, **-án** or **-en** in the present tense.

You use **ellos/ellas** (third person plural) to translate *they*. Use **ellos** to refer to more than one masculine person or thing, or to a mixture of masculine and feminine people or things. Only use **ellas** if all the people or things are feminine. After **ellos/ellas** the verb usually ends in **-an**, **-án** or **-en** in the present tense.

3.2 Lo, la, los, las – him, her, it, them: direct object pronouns

▶▶ **If you know what a direct object pronoun is and how to use it, go on to 3.3.**

Him, her and *it* are called object pronouns. They stand for the person who or object which has the action done to it.

I saw John/*him*.
John saw Karen/*her*.
I bought the watch/*it*.
I like Paul/*him*.
He likes Isabelle/*her*.
She doesn't like the boys/*them*.

I Which is the direct object?

a I bought a new car.
b My husband drove it home for me.
c A dog chased a cat across the road.
d He swerved and hit a tree.
e He broke the wing mirror.
f He bought me a bunch of flowers.
g He took the car to the garage to be repaired.

3.2.1 Lo, la, los, las – him, her, it, them, you

The words for *him, her, it, them, you* (formal form) in Spanish are as follows:

| | singular | | plural | |
	masc	fem	masc	fem
you (formal)	lo (le)	la	los (les)	las
him, her, them	lo (le)	la	los (les)	las
it, them	lo	la	los	las

The words for *him/her/it* and *them* in Spanish are **lo/los** (masculine) and **la/las** (feminine), and these words are also used to refer to *you* (formal: **usted** in the singular and **ustedes** in the plural). In some parts of Spain **le** and **les** are used instead of **lo** and **los** for *people only*. **La** is *always* used for female people and feminine nouns.

In Spanish, the **lo, la, le, los, las** and **les** usually come in front of the verb. However, when there is more than one verb together (for instance, a participle or an infinitive along with the verb), they can be tacked onto the end of the infinitive or participle. They also have to be tacked onto the end of a positive command. This sometimes means that the verb needs an accent to keep the stress in the right place.

Ya lo veo.	I can see him/it (lit: him/it I see).
No los veo.	I don't see them (lit: not them I see).
Le llamaré esta tarde.	I'll call you this afternoon.
Queremos comerlas/Las queremos comer.	We want to eat them.
Están comprándola/La están comprando.	They are buying it.
No podemos llamarlas en seguida.	We can't call them immediately.
¡Bébelo!	Drink it!
¡No lo olvides!	Don't you forget it!

I Señora Ramos buys a new skirt (**la falda**). Marcos bought some socks (**los calcetines**). What is the pronoun?

a Señora Ramos sees two nice skirts.	_____ ve.
b She buys one.	_____ compra.
c She takes it home.	_____ lleva a casa.
d She wears it this evening.	_____ lleva puesta esta tarde.
e Señor Ramos finds it old-fashioned.	El señor Ramos _____ encuentra pasada de moda.
f She takes it back to the shop.	_____ devuelve a la tienda.
g Marcos saw some nice socks and bought them.	Marcos vio unos calcetines bonitos y _____ compró.
h He put them in his bag.	_____ puso en su bolsa.
i On the way home, he left it on the bus.	Camino de casa _____ dejó olvidada en el autobús.

3.2.2 *Me, te, nos, os* – me, you, us

	singular	**plural**
me, us	me	nos
you (familiar)	te	os

These pronouns are used in the same way as **lo**, **la**, etc. (see 3.2.1), so they also usually come in front of the verb.

No me olvides.	Don't forget me.
Ya te veo.	I can see you now.
Nunca nos llaman.	They never call us.
Os visitaré pasado mañana.	I'll visit you the day after tomorrow.
No quiere verme.	She doesn't want to see me.

I Answer these questions, changing **me** to **te**, **nos** to **os** and vice versa as necessary.

a Oye, ¿me quieres? Sí ____ quiero.
b ¿Puedo besarte? No, no ____ puedes besar.
c ¿Vais a llamarnos? Sí, ____ llamaremos mañana.
d ¿Podemos visitaros mañana? Si, podéis visitar____ mañana.

3.2.3 ▶Fast track: Direct object pronouns

Lo, la, le, los, las, les – him, her, it, them, you

In English *him, her, you, it*, etc. almost always come straight after the verb.

In Spanish, **lo**, **la**, **le**, **los**, **las**, **les**, etc. normally come in front of the verb.

Lo/Le vi en la calle.	I saw him in the street.
Las quiero mucho.	I love them lots.
Los/Les veré mañana.	I'll see you tomorrow.

Le and **les** are used for people by some Spanish speakers.

Me, te, nos, os – me, you, us

¿Me viste llegar?	Did you see me arrive?
¡Te odio!	I hate you!
Nos enfadaste al hacer esto.	You annoyed us when you did that.
Os dejamos y nos vamos a casa.	We are leaving you and going home.

I Answer these questions using **me**, **te**, **nos** and **os** as appropriate.

a ¿Quieres que te llame esta tarde? Sí, lláma____.
b ¿Queréis visitarnos el domingo? No, no ____ visitaremos.
c ¿Me presentas a tu novia? Sí, ____ la presento.
d Os veré mañana, ¿vale? Sí, ven a ver____ mañana.

3.3 *Me, te, le, nos, os, les*: indirect object pronouns

▶▶ **If you know what an indirect object pronoun is and how to use it, go on to 3.4.**

In English, an indirect object pronoun is the same as a direct object pronoun but has (or can have) *to* or *for* in front of it.

- *I bought her it. I bought it* (direct object – it is the thing that you bought) *for her* (indirect object).
- *Give me it. Give it* (direct object – the thing which is being given) *to me* (indirect object).
- *They showed him it. They showed it* (direct object – the thing which is being shown) *to him* (indirect object).

The indirect object pronouns in Spanish are as follows:

singular	plural
me – (to) me	nos – (to) us
te – (to) you	os – (to) you
le – (to) him/her/you (formal)	les – (to) them/you (formal)

 Indirect pronouns are used with verbs such as *give, send, write, show, buy, offer, tell, lend,* where you do something *to/for* someone/something.

I Identify the indirect object pronouns in these English sentences.

 Try saying *to/for* in front of the pronoun to see if it is indirect.

- **a** Pascual sent me a text message.
- **b** I could not read it. My friend can. I showed it to her.
- **c** She translated it for me.
- **d** I wrote him a reply.
- **e** She sent it for me.
- **f** He sent her a new message.
- **g** She did not show me it.

h She sent him a photo of herself.
i He sent her another message.
j She sent him a reply.
k He texted her.
l She did not tell me what he said.
m She gave me my phone back and went.

3.3.1 Word order: indirect object pronouns

In Spanish, the indirect object pronoun usually comes in front of the verb.

Exceptions: it can be placed on the end of an infinitive or a participle, and it must be tacked onto the end of a positive command.

¿Me pasas esa manzana?	Will you pass (to) me that apple?
Te mandaré diez euros.	I'll send (to) you ten euros.
Le devolverán su coche pronto.	They'll soon return her car to her.
Le digo que no puede entrar.	I tell (to) you, you can't go in.
Por favor, mándenos un mensaje.	Please send (to) us a message.
¡Os digo que no podéis jugar al fútbol aquí!	I tell you, you can't play football here!
Voy a ofrecerles un premio.	I am going to offer you a prize.
Salió sin decirles adiós.	He went out without saying goodbye to them.

Me, te, nos and **os** are the same as the direct object pronouns, so you only have to remember **le** – *to you* (formal singular form), *to him/her* and **les** – *to you* (formal plural form), *to them*.

I Finish off these sentences, adding the appropriate indirect object pronoun as indicated.

– Hijo, no (**to you**) hablamos con frecuencia. Ven aquí: tienes que prestar (**to me**) atención. ¿Por qué no (**to us**) escribiste para explicar? Vamos a dar (**to you**) un consejo. Deberías mandar (**to her**) unas flores. Cuando vayas a casa de sus padres, deberías ofrecer (**to them**) una botella de vino.

– Mamá y papá, (**to you**) he escuchado. Pero basta ya: no quiero hablar (**to her**) más.

3.3.2 Word order: direct and indirect object pronouns

▶▶ **If you don't need to know about this yet, go on to 3.3.3.**

If there is more than one object pronoun together in a sentence, the indirect object pronoun comes before the direct object pronoun. Remember that **me, te, nos** and **os** can be either direct or indirect object pronouns.

The only slight complication is that, if the indirect object pronouns **le** and **les** are followed by a third person object pronoun, the indirect object pronoun (which will usually be a person) changes to **se**. This is purely to avoid two pronouns beginning with **l-** coming together.

yo		me	me	
tú		te	te	
él		le*	lo/le	
ella		le*	la	
usted		le*	le/lo/la	
nosotros/as	(no)	nos	nos	(verb)
vosotros/as		os	os	
ellos		les*	les/los/las	
ellas		les*	les/los/las	
ustedes		les*	les/los/las	

* If these are followed by **lo/le/la** or **les/los/las**, they change to **se**.

Note that these rules apply whether the pronouns are in front of the verb or tacked onto the end of an infinitive, a participle or a positive command.

 Choose a sentence to memorise to help you remember the sound of the phrases.

Me lo dio ayer.	She gave it to me yesterday.
Te los mandaré mañana.	I'll send them to you tomorrow.
Se las devuelvo en seguida.	I'll give them back to you straight away.
Quiero devolvérselas en seguida.	I want to give them back to you straight away.
¡Dámelos en seguida!	Give them to me immediately!

I   How would you say the following?

a My friend gave them to me.   Mi amigo ____ dio.
b Please send it to them.   Por favor, mánde____.
c When did she tell it to them?   ¿Cuándo ____ contó?
d I can't give them to you.   No puedo dár____.
e Ladies, I can tell it to you now. Señoras, puedo contár ____
                                        ahora.

▶▶ **If you have had enough of pronouns, move on to Chapter 4 on Adjectives and come back later.**

3.3.3   ▶**Fast track:** Indirect object pronouns

In English, an indirect object pronoun is the same as a direct object pronoun but has (or can have) *to* or *for* in front of it.

Indirect object pronouns are used with verbs such as *give, send, write, show, buy, offer, tell, lend,* where you do something *to/for* someone.

 The indirect object pronouns are very similar to the direct object pronouns!

me	to me
te	to you (familiar singular)
le	to him/her/it
le	to you (formal singular)
nos	to us
os	to you
les	to them
les	to you (formal plural)

In Spanish, indirect object pronouns go in the same place as direct object pronouns. To sum up, this is:

• usually immediately in front of the verb
• optionally on the end of an infinitive or present participle
• compulsorily on the end of a positive command.

If you have more than one pronoun, either in front of the verb or on the end of it, the indirect object pronoun always comes before the direct object pronoun.

Se lo di.   I gave it to her.
Nos la dieron en la escuela.   They gave it to us at school.

Te la doy en seguida.	I will give it to you immediately.
Me lo mandarás, ¿no?	You will send it to me, won't you?
¿Por qué no se las devuelves?	Why don't you give them back to them?
Tienen ustedes que devolvérmelo.	You have to give it back to me.
¡Dámelo ahora!	Give it to me now!

I   Complete the sentences with the necessary pronouns.

a Su madre ____ regaló. (it to me)
b Hágame el favor de quitár____ . (it off you)
c ¿Cuándo ____ envió? (them to us)
d No puedo explicár____. (it to her)
e Señores, aquí tienen sus chalecos salvavidas: póngan____ ahora.
(them on you)

 You can easily avoid having to use more than one pronoun by repeating one of the nouns!

3.4 *Mí, ti,* etc.: prepositional/disjunctive pronouns

Prepositional or disjunctive pronouns are used after prepositions (see 6.1), but only when talking about people or animals. Most of them are the same as the subject pronouns. The exceptions are: **mí**, **ti** and **sí**.

con él – with him, sin ella – without her, para ellos – for them, cerca de nosotros – around us, delante de ellas – in front of them.

Este libro es para ti.	This book is for you.
Quiero ir a Madrid con ellas.	I want to go to Madrid with them.
¿Es para usted?	Is it for you?
Es con ella.	He's with her.
Compramos un regalo para él.	We're buying a present for him.
¿Vamos con ustedes?	Are we going with you?

There are three special forms: **conmigo** and **contigo**, which are used in the singular for *with me* and *with you* (familiar form), and **consigo**, which is only used for true reflexive situations.

mí	me
ti	you (familiar singular)
él	him/it
ella	her/it
sí	...self (only used for a true reflexive situation)
usted	you (formal singular)
nosotros/as	us
vosotros/as	you (familiar plural)
ellos/ellas	them
sí	...selves (only used for a true reflexive situation)
ustedes	you (formal plural)

I Replace the people in italics or complete the sentence with a pronoun after the preposition.

a Tengo que hablar con *mi amigo*.
b Me gusta estar al lado de *mi querida Carmen*.
c Vamos a la playa con *nuestras amigas*.
d Lo siento, este billete no pone su nombre: no es para *Ramón Ramos*.
e Miguel, este libro es para _____.
f Rosi y Marta, esta invitación es para _____.
g Señoritas, la estación está detrás de _____.
h Mis padres me regalaron este coche a _____.
i ¡Qué suerte! querido, hemos ganado la lotería: este premio es para _____.

3.5 Object pronouns and the imperative

▶▶ **If you are not going to be telling people what to do, leave this out and go on to 3.6.**

You probably already know the parts of this that you are likely to need. Check that it looks familiar and then move on.

When used with a verb in the positive imperative form, the object pronoun has to be added to the end of the verb, which may need an accent on the stressed syllable to keep the stress in the right place.

Cómelo todo.	Eat it all.
Levántelas.	Lift them up.
Mírame.	Look at me.

Tómelo.	Hold it.
Escogedla.	Choose it.
¡Dígame!	Tell me.

singular	plural
¡mírame!	¡míranos!
¡mírale!	¡mírales!
¡míralo!	¡míralos!
¡mírala!	¡míralas!

I How would you say: look at ...?

Míra ...

a us
b him
c them (feminine)
d it (feminine)
e me

3.5.1 Pronouns with reflexive verbs in the imperative

lávate	wash yourself (familiar singular)
lávese	wash yourself (formal singular)
lavaos	wash yourselves (familiar plural)
lávense	wash yourselves (formal plural)

I Tell the people in brackets to have a wash!

a (2 friends) Lav___
b (1 stranger) Láv____
c (1 friend) Láv____

3.5.2 Order of pronouns in the imperative

If there is more than one object pronoun added to the end of the imperative, the indirect object pronoun always comes before the direct object pronoun.

Dámelo.	Give it to me.
Cómpramelas.	Buy them for me.
Devuélvanoslo.	Give it back to us.

3.6 ¿Quién? ¿Qué?: interrogative words

An interrogative word is used to ask questions such as *who, why, how, which?* Most are either pronouns or adverbs. Here are some common ones, with their meanings.

 **If you know all about interrogatives, go on to 3.7.**

¿Quién/Quiénes? – *who(m):* this word means *who* if it refers to the subject of the sentence and *whom* if it refers to the object.

 Remember, the subject is the person who or thing which 'does' the action.

¿Quién es esta mujer?	Who is this woman?
¿Con quién estás?	Who(m) are you with?
¿Quiénes son estas personas?	Who are these people?

¿De quiénes? – *whose:* this expression means *whose* when it is used to ask a question. (NB: the word **cuyo/a/os/as** is used for *whose* as a relative pronoun; see 3.8.4.)

¿De quién es este coche?	Whose car is this?
¿De quién es el hermano?	Whose brother is he?
¿De quiénes son estos abrigos?	Whose are these coats?

¿Qué? – *what, which:* **qué** usually means *what,* but it can mean *which* if used with a noun.

¿Qué es?	What is it?
¿Qué vas a comer?	What are you going to eat?
¿Qué coche es el mejor?	Which car is the best?

¿Cuál/Cuáles? – *which:* this word is used if there is a choice between two or more things. **Cuál** is the singular and **cuáles** is the plural.

Hay dos libros. ¿Cuál prefieres?	There are two books. Which do you prefer?
Tiene tres hermanas. ¿Cuáles están aquí?	He has three sisters. Which ones are here?

¿Cuánto/a? ¿Cuántos/as? – *how much, how many:* used as an adjective or a pronoun, this agrees with the noun(s) it refers to. It is sometimes used as an adverb, in which case it doesn't change.

As an adjective or a pronoun:

¿Cuánto dinero tienes?	How much money have you got?
¿Cuánta cerveza quieres?	How much beer do you want?
¿Cuántos hermanos tienes?	How many brothers have you got?
¿Cuántas casas hay en la ciudad? ¿Cuántas hay en tu calle?	How many houses are there in the city? How many are there in your street?

As an adverb meaning *how much*:

¿Cuánto vale?	How much is it?

I Complete these questions with the appropriate form of **¿cuánto?**

a ¿____ amigas vienen a tu fiesta?
b ¿____ carne hay en la nevera?
c Necesito unos huevos. ¿____ necesitas?
d Vamos a beber vino. ¿____ tenemos?
e ¿____ tortillas vas a preparar?

3.7 *Mío, tuyo,* etc.: possessive pronouns

▶▶ **If you want to avoid using the possessive pronouns for the moment, you can say 'de Miguel', etc. (see section 3.4). Go on to 3.8.**

mine	(el) mío	(la) mía	(los) míos	(las) mías
yours (familiar sing.)	(el) tuyo	(la) tuya	(los) tuyos	(las) tuyas
his/hers/its	(el) suyo	(la) suya	(los) suyos	(las) suyas
yours (formal sing.)	(el) suyo	(la) suya	(los) suyos	(las) suyas
ours	(el) nuestro	(la) nuestra	(los) nuestros	(las) nuestras
yours (familiar pl.)	(el) vuestro	(la) vuestra	(los) vuestros	(las) vuestras
theirs (masc. and fem.)	(el) suyo	(la) suya	(los) suyos	(las) suyas
yours (formal pl.)	(el) suyo	(la) suya	(los) suyos	(las) suyas

Possessive pronouns translate the English *mine, yours, his, hers, ours, yours, theirs*. They have to agree with the noun they are replacing, and are used with the definite article except after the verb **ser** – *to be:* **es mío** – *it's mine.*

I Replace the nouns in italics with the correct form of the pronoun: (**el**) **mío**, (**la**) **mía**, (**los**) **míos**, (**las**) **mías**.

a Aquí tienes *tu cartera*, pero, ¿dónde está _____?
b No quiero *tus discos*, quiero escuchar _____
c ¿Por qué sales con *mi paraguas*? Coge el tuyo y dame _____
d Me gustan *estas gafas*, pero prefiero _____
e Acabo de encontrar *unas fotos*. Parece que son _____
f Ésta es *mi carta*. Es _____
g Éstos son *mis periódicos*. Son _____
h Voy a prestarte *este abrigo*. Es _____

II Replace the nouns in italics with the correct form of the pronoun: **el suyo**, **la suya**, **los suyos**, **las suyas** (NB: a couple here are for **usted(es)**).

a ¿Son *las gafas* de Juan? Sí, acaba de comprar _____
b Dime cuál es *el hijo* de doña Juana. Creo que _____ no está aquí.
c Nosotros compraremos *nuestros billetes*, y ustedes comprarán _____, ¿verdad?
d ¿Sabes dónde está *la casa* de los señores Rodríguez? Sí, _____ está al final de la calle.
e Don José, ¿*este coche* es de usted, es _____?
f ¿*Esta niña* es de María? No, no es _____
g Severiano no quiere ponerse *estos pantalones*, pues no son _____
h Tuve que pedir prestadas *unas tazas* a la vecina, pues éstas son _____

III Replace the nouns in italics with the correct form of the pronoun: **el vuestro**, **la vuestra**, **los vuestros**, **las vuestras**.

a Juancho y Paqui, quiero ver *los periódicos*; ¿puedo leer _____?
b No nos gusta nada *nuestro padre*, preferimos _____
c ¿Dónde está *vuestra casa*? ¿Es ésta _____?
d Acabo de encontrar *unas revistas*: ¿habéis perdido _____?
e *Estos billetes* son de vosotros, ¿no? Son _____
f ¿Cuál de *estas televisiones* es _____?
g Merche y Anita, *estas manzanas* son _____ ¿verdad?
h Niños, encontré *un balón*. ¿Es _____?

3.8 *Que, quien*, etc.: relative pronouns

▶▶ **If you can recognise a relative pronoun, go on to 3.8.1.**

Relative pronouns are the words *who, which* and *whose* when they are used to refer to someone or something already mentioned. Some of them look like the question words, but they do not have accents. They also serve a different purpose – they link sentences, but they do not ask questions. **Quien** is only used after prepositions, and only for people.

La mujer *que* vive en Madrid	The woman *who* lives in Madrid
El perro *que* ladra todos los días	The dog *which/that* barks every day
Mi ordenador *que* no funciona	My computer *which/that* doesn't work
El hombre con *quien* he venido	The man with *whom* I came ('the man I came with')
El coche, en *el cual* he salido	The car in *which* I left ('which I left in')
El hombre *cuyo* coche está siempre aparcado delante de nuestra casa	The man *whose* car is always parked in front of our house

The part of the sentence that contains the relative pronoun is called a relative clause, one of various types of subordinate clause.

 A 'subordinate clause' is a name for part of a sentence which doesn't make sense on its own but depends on the rest of the sentence to complete its meaning.

3.8.1 *Que* – who, which, that

You can use **que** for *who, whom, which* or *that* in most situations, to refer to people or things. You can't use it if you are talking about a person and there is a preposition before the pronoun – i.e. *to whom* (or *who ... to*), *for whom* (or *who ... for*).

El hombre *que* vi ayer	The man (*who(m)*) I saw yesterday
La botella *que* rompió	The bottle (*that*) he broke

3.8.2 *Quien(es)* – (with, for, etc.) whom

You use **quien** when you are talking about a person and there is a preposition before the pronoun – i.e. *to whom* (or *who ... to*), *for whom* (or *who ... for*). **Quien** is used after the so-called *personal a*, which is needed with names of people or any word which defines them.

El amigo para *quien* he traído este regalo	The friend for whom I have brought this present ('The friend I have brought this present for')

Las mujeres con *quienes* he llegado	The women with whom I arrived ('The women I arrived with')
Ésta es la chica *a quien* conocí en la discoteca	This is the girl I met at the disco
No sé a *quienes* te refieres, pero no son esos hombres.	I don't know who you are referring to, but it is not those men.

3.8.3 *El cual*, etc. – who/whom/which

You can use **el cual/la cual/los cuales/las cuales** when you are talking about a person or a thing, and you can also use it when there is a preposition before the pronoun – i.e. *to whom* (or *who ... to*), *for whom* (or *who ... for*).
It must agree in gender and number with the noun it refers to.

La silla, al lado de *la cual* estaba sentado el gato	The chair beside which the cat was sitting ('The chair the cat was sitting beside')
El tejado, sobre *el cual* la policía ha descubierto al criminal	The roof on which the police discovered the criminal ('The roof the police discovered the criminal on')
Los soldados, contra *los cuales* luchan	The soldiers against whom they are fighting ('The soldiers they are fighting against')
Las casas, detrás de *las cuales* están los árboles	The houses behind which are the trees ('The houses the trees are behind')

3.8.4 *Cuyo/a*, *cuyos/as* – whose

You use **cuyo/cuya/cuyos/cuyas** when you want to say *whose*. The word has to agree in gender and number with the noun it refers to.

El coche *cuyo* motor es ruidoso.	The car whose engine is noisy
La princesa *cuya* nariz es grande.	The princess whose nose is big
El hombre *cuyos* niños son pesados	The man whose children are irritating
El hotel *cuyas* habitaciones son caras	The hotel whose rooms are expensive

I   Complete the sentences using the appropriate form of **que**, **quien**, **el cual** or **cuyo** as best fits the meaning of the sentence.

a ¿Quién es la chica ____ vi en el parque?
Who is the girl I saw in the park?

b No conozco a la señora ____ vive aquí.
I don't know the woman who lives here.

c No sé ____ dirigirme sobre todo esto.
I don't know who to talk to about all this.

d Éste es el chico ____ coche me atropelló.
This is the boy whose car ran me over.

e Es una persona de ____ no sé nada.
She is a person about whom I know nothing.

f Busco a un español ____ vive en Roma.
I'm looking for a Spanish man who lives in Rome.

3.9 Éste/ésta, ése/ésa, aquél/aquélla – this, that, etc.

There are three demonstrative pronouns in Spanish which do the same job as *this* and *that* in English. They agree in number and gender with the noun they are referring to, and each has a different function according to how far away the object being referred to is from the person who is speaking.

When you would use *this* in English (i.e. for something right next to you), use **éste/ésta** (etc.). For something that is a bit further away, but is still near you, use **ése/ésa** (etc.). Finally, for things that are even further away, use **aquél/aquélla** (etc.). Here is a table of all three words in all their forms. In practice, Spanish people use **éste** and **aquél** most, and **ése** comes in useful when all three pronouns are needed together.

meaning	singular		plural	
	masculine	feminine	masculine	feminine
this (next to you)	éste	ésta	éstos	éstas
that (near you)	ése	ésa	ésos	ésas
that (further away)	aquél	aquélla	aquéllos	aquéllas

¿Cuál de los anillos prefieres?	Which ring do you prefer?
Prefiero éste. Tú prefieres aquél, ¿verdad?	I prefer this one (here). You prefer that one (there), don't you.
¿Cuáles de las flores prefieres?	Which flowers do you prefer?
Yo prefiero éstas, y tú prefieres ésas, ¿verdad? Pero mi madre prefiere aquéllas.	I prefer these, and you prefer those, don't you? But my mother prefers those over there.

I Say you want to order *these* things.

Para la boda, quiero ...
a un novio hermoso
b unas damas de honor
c un traje de novia
d una alianza de oro
e un collar de plata
f una diadema bonita
g unos pendientes de plata
h un ramo de flores
i unos zapatos blancos
j unos guantes blancos

II Say you want *those* things, using **ése** or **aquél**.

... y como regalos ...
a unas sábanas
b una cama cómoda
c unas mantas
d un espejo
e unos manteles
f un armario grande
g una cocina de gas
h un congelador
i una batería de cocina
j unos vasos bonitos

3.10 ▶Fast track: Pronouns

A pronoun is a word which stands for a noun.

Subject pronouns

A subject pronoun stands for the person who or thing which does the action described by a verb: *I, you ...* etc.

They can be used in front of verbs and to replace a person or thing you have already mentioned. In Spanish they are often missed out because the verb ending does their job (which is to show who or what the verb is referring to).

They are:

singular		plural	
yo	I	nosotros/as	we
tú	you (familiar)	vosotros/as	you (familiar)
él	he	ellos	they (m)
ella	she	ellas	they (f)
usted	you (formal)	ustedes	you (formal)

Direct object pronouns: me, you, etc.

A direct object pronoun stands in for the person who or object which has the action done to it.

They are:

singular		plural	
me	me	nos	us
te	you (familiar)	os	you (familiar)
le/lo	him/it	les/los	them (m)
la	her/it	las	them (f)
le/lo/la	you (formal)	les/los/las	you (formal)

In English, they come after the verb. In Spanish they come in front of the verb, except that they can be put on the end of present participles and infinitives. They also *must* be put on the end of positive commands.

Le veo.	I see him. (lit: him I see.)
Ella me ve.	She sees me. (lit: She me sees.)
Yo lo veo.	I see him/it. (lit: I him see.)
No les vemos.	We don't see them. (lit: Not them we see.)

 In the perfect tense the pronouns always come before the part of **haber**.

Indirect object pronouns: to me, to him, etc.

In English, the indirect object pronouns are the same as the direct object pronouns, but have (or can have) *to* or *for* in front of them. In Spanish, there is a special set of them, but it is very similar to the set of direct object pronouns.

They are:

singular	plural
me – to me	nos – to us
te – to you (familiar)	os – to you (familiar)
le – to him/her/it	les – to them
le – to you (formal)	les – to you (formal)

 Most of these are the same as the direct object pronouns.

If you have more than one pronoun, either in front of the verb or on the end of it, the indirect object pronoun always goes first.

yo		me	me	
tú		te	te	
él		le	lo/le	
ella		le	la	
usted		le	le/lo/la	
nosotros/as	(no)	nos	nos	(verb)
vosotros/as		os	os	
ellos		les	les/los/las	
ellas		les	les/los/las	
ustedes		les	les/los/las	

NB: When two third person pronouns together would both begin with **l-**, the indirect pronoun, usually referring to a person, is changed to **se**.

Disjunctive pronouns

The disjunctive (or prepositional) pronouns are used after prepositions, e.g. *for me, with us*: **para mí**; **con nosotros**.

There are three special forms: **conmigo** and **contigo**, which are used in the singular for *with me* and *with you* (familiar form), and **consigo**, which is only used for true reflexive situations.

The usual forms are as follows:

singular	plural
mí – me	nosotros/as – us
ti – you (familiar)	vosotros/as – you (familiar)
él – him/it	ellos – them (m)
ella – her/it	ellas – them (f)
sí – ...self	sí – ...selves
usted – you (formal)	ustedes – you (formal)

Interrogative words

Most interrogative words are pronouns or adverbs. They are used to ask questions like *Who?* or *What?*

¿Quién(es)?	who? (referring to the subject of a sentence or clause)
¿Quién(es)?	whom? (referring to the object of a sentence or clause)
¿De quién(es)?	whose?
¿Qué?	what?, which?
¿Cuál? ¿Cuáles?	which?, which one?
¿Cuánto/a? ¿Cuántos/as?	how much?, how many?

Mío, tuyo – mine, yours, etc.

These are called possessive pronouns. They translate the English *mine, yours, his, hers, ours, yours, theirs*. They have to agree with the noun they are replacing.

mine	el mío	la mía	los míos	las mías
yours (familiar sing.)	el tuyo	la tuya	los tuyos	las tuyas
his/hers/its	el suyo	la suya	los suyos	las suyas
yours (formal sing.)	el suyo	la suya	los suyos	las suyas
ours	el nuestro	la nuestra	los nuestros	las nuestras
yours (familiar pl.)	el vuestro	la vuestra	los vuestros	las vuestras
theirs (masc. and fem.)	el suyo	la suya	los suyos	las suyas
yours (formal pl.)	el suyo	la suya	los suyos	las suyas

Que, quien, el cual, cuyo – who, whose, which

These are called relative pronouns. They translate *who, that, which* and *whose* when they are used to refer to someone or something already mentioned.

que	who/whom, which, that
quien	(with, for, etc.) whom
el/la cual, los/las cuales	who/whom, which
cuyo/a, cuyos/as	whose

éste/ésta, ése/ésa, aquél/aquélla – this, that, etc.

These are called demonstrative pronouns. **Éste/esta** translates *this* and **aquél/aquélla** translates *that*, but there is an extra word (**ése/ésa**) for things that are not right next to you and not a long way away (so they are quite near).

singular		plural	
masc	**fem**	**masc**	**fem**
éste	ésta	éstos	éstas
ése	ésa	ésos	ésas
aquél	aquélla	aquéllos	aquéllas

4 ADJECTIVES

What is an adjective?

▶▶ **If you know what an adjective is, go on to 4.1.**

Adjectives are 'describing' words. You use them to say what something or someone is like.

I Highlight the adjectives in these sentences.

a Peter is short and fat.
b She has long, blond hair and green eyes.
c He has just bought a new computer.
d She likes to wear new clothes for parties and casual clothes for gardening.
e Her car is large and old and has four-wheel drive.
f Her boyfriend is tall and dark.
g She manages a small insurance company.
h He has an older sister and a younger brother.
i Her favourite dish is paella.
j He likes his beer very cold.

4.1 Adjectival agreement

In Spanish, the adjective 'agrees' with the noun. Most singular adjectives end in **-o** when they are used with a masculine noun, and these change their ending to **-a** with a feminine noun.

 There are adjectives which don't work quite like this.

▶▶ **If you know about adjectival agreement, go on to 4.3 Fast track.**

| | singular | | plural | |
	masculine	**feminine**	**masculine**	**feminine**
new	nuevo	nueva	nuevos	nuevas
old	antiguo	antigua	antiguos	antiguas

I Fill in the right form of **nuevo, nueva, nuevos, nuevas** or **antiguo, antigua, antiguos, antiguas** (your choice).

a un coche _____
b una casa _____
c sombreros _____
d sillas _____
e un tren _____
f una televisión _____
g ordenadores _____
h ciudades _____

4.1.1   Adjectives ending in **-o**

Most adjectives end in **-o** in the masculine singular and change as follows:

• If the noun is masculine singular, the adjective ends in **-o**: **nuevo, antiguo**.
• If the noun is feminine singular, the adjective ends in **-a**: **nueva, antigua**.
• If the noun is masculine plural, the adjective ends in **-os**. **nuevos, antiguos**.
• If the noun is feminine plural, the adjective ends in **-as**. **nuevas, antiguas**.

meaning	singular		plural	
	masculine	feminine	masculine	feminine
new	nuevo	nueva	nuevos	nuevas
little	pequeño	pequeña	pequeños	pequeñas
good	bueno	buena	buenos	buenas
white	blanco	blanca	blancos	blancas

4.1.2   Adjectives ending in **-e**

If an adjective ends in **-e**, it doesn't change between the masculine and feminine singular. However, it does have an **-s** on the end in the masculine and feminine plural:

meaning	singular		plural	
	masculine	feminine	masculine	feminine
green	verde	verde	verdes	verdes
strong	fuerte	fuerte	fuertes	fuertes

4.1.3 Adjectives ending in a consonant

If an adjective ends in a consonant, again it doesn't change in the singular, but it has **-es** on the end in the masculine and feminine plural (this is to make it easier to say, because an **s** after a consonant would often be difficult to pronounce).

	singular		plural	
meaning	**masculine**	**feminine**	**masculine**	**feminine**
blue	azul	azul	azules	azules
weak	débil	débil	débiles	débiles

4.1.4 Other patterns

If an adjective ends in **-ete** or **-ote**, the **-e** becomes **-a** in the feminine singular, and **-s** is added to both of these to make the plural forms.

	singular		plural	
meaning	**masculine**	**feminine**	**masculine**	**feminine**
chubby	regordete	regordeta	regordetes	regordetas

If an adjective ends in **-a**, both singular forms are the same (because you obviously couldn't add another **a** in the feminine!), and **-s** is added to make the plural.

	singular		plural	
meaning	**masculine**	**feminine**	**masculine**	**feminine**
cycling	ciclista	ciclista	ciclistas	ciclistas
Communist	comunista	comunista	comunistas	comunistas

If an adjective ends in **-án**, **-ín**, **-ón** or **-or**, it has a separate feminine form ending in **-a**, and different plural forms for masculine (**-es**) and feminine (**-as**). Note that when there is an accent on the last syllable of the adjective in the masculine form, it disappears in the feminine and plural.

	singular		plural	
meaning	**masculine**	**feminine**	**masculine**	**feminine**
lazy	holgazán	holgazana	holgazanes	holgazanas
chatty	parlanchín	parlanchina	parlanchines	parlanchinas
grumpy	gruñón	gruñona	gruñones	gruñonas
hard-working	trabajador	trabajadora	trabajadores	trabajadoras

I Fill the gaps in the table.

		singular		plural	
	meaning	**masculine**	**feminine**	**masculine**	**feminine**
a	happy	feliz	feliz	felices	felices
b	sad	triste	triste	tristes	tristes
c	short	corto	corta	cortos	cortas
d	tall/big	grande	___	grandes	grandes
e	weak	___	débil	débiles	débiles
f	strong	fuerte	fuerte	fuertes	fuertes
g	intelligent	inteligente	inteligente	___	inteligentes
h	stupid	estúpido	estúpida	estúpidos	estúpidas
i	pretty	guapo	___	guapos	guapas
j	easy	fácil	fácil	___	fáciles
k	polite	cortés	cortés	corteses	corteses
l	good	bueno	buena	buenos	buenas
m	bad	malo	___	malos	malas
n	young	joven	joven	jóvenes	___
o	wide	ancho	ancha	anchos	anchas
p	thin	delgado	___	delgados	delgadas
q	hard-working	trabajador	trabajadora	trabajadores	___
r	clean	limpio	limpia	limpios	limpias
s	dirty	sucio	sucia	sucios	sucias
t	friendly	amistoso	amistosa	___	amistosas

II Give the right form of the adjectives in brackets.

a Mi tío es ____ (gordo)
b Mi tía no es ____ (gordo)
c Mi hermana es ____ (holgazán)
d Mis padres no son ____ (bueno)
e Mi hermano es ____ (trabajador)
f Su amiga no es ____ (trabajador)
g Mis amigas son ____ (bueno)
h Mis abuelos son ____ (bueno)
i ¡Este agua no es ____! (natural)
j Las fotos son _____ (natural)
k Granada es una ciudad ____ (viejo)
l El Señor Ramírez es un profesor de español ____ (viejo)
m La Haya es la capital de los Países ____ (Bajo)
n La silla es demasiado ____ (bajo)
o Es una casa ____ (nuevo)
p Hay un hotel ____ en esta calle. (nuevo)
q Los televisores ____ son muy ____ (nuevo, caro)

r Esta calle es muy ____ (ancho)
s Tenemos un coche ____ (grande)
t Mis notas son ____ (bueno)

4.1.5 Adjectives of nationality

Most adjectives of nationality or regional origin end in an **-o** or a consonant. These all end in **-a** in the feminine singular (replacing the **-o** if there was one), whilst the masculine plurals end in **-os** or **-es** as appropriate, and the feminine plurals end in **-as**. The accent on the masculine singular form, if any, is not needed on the other forms. Nationalities which end in **-a** and **-e** don't change in the singular, but add **-s** in the plural; the few ending in **-í** only add **-es** for the plural. Note that adjectives of nationality do not begin with a capital letter.

meaning	singular		plural	
	masculine	**feminine**	**masculine**	**feminine**
Italian	italiano	italiana	italianos	italianas
Swiss	suizo	suiza	suizos	suizas
Russian	ruso	rusa	rusos	rusas
American	americano	americana	americanos	americanas
Spanish	español	española	españoles	españolas
German	alemán	alemana	alemanes	alemanas
French	francés	francesa	franceses	francesas
Scottish	escocés	escocesa	escoceses	escocesas
English	inglés	inglesa	ingleses	inglesas
Belgian	belga	belga	belgas	belgas
Canadian	canadiense	canadiense	canadienses	canadienses
Moroccan	marroquí	marroquí	marroquíes	marroquíes

VI Fill in the nationalities in the correct form.

a Michael Schumacher es ____
b Jensen Button es ____
c Madonna es ____
d Pedro Almodóvar es ____
e Plácido Domingo y José Carreras son ____
f Tim Henman y Kelly Holmes son ____
g Luciano Pavarotti es ____
h Tom y Martha viven en Washington: son ____
i Billy Connolly es ____
j Estos señores son de Montreal – son ____

4.1.6 Colours

Most adjectives of colour agree in the same way as other adjectives, and they always come after the noun they describe: *a red car* becomes *a car red:* **un coche rojo**; *the White House* becomes *the house white:* **la Casa Blanca**.

 Choose a phrase to memorise to help you remember the order: **un sombrero blanco**; **un gato negro**, for example.

meaning	singular		plural	
	masculine	feminine	masculine	feminine
red	rojo	roja	rojos	rojas
yellow	amarillo	amarilla	amarillos	amarillas
blue	azul	azul	azules	azules
green	verde	verde	verdes	verdes
black	negro	negra	negros	negras
white	blanco	blanca	blancos	blancas
grey	gris	gris	grises	grises
pink	rosado	rosada	rosados	rosadas
brown	marrón	marrón	marrones	marrones
orange	naranja	naranja	naranja	naranja
purple	violeta	violeta	violeta	violeta

Most adjectives of colour form their agreements using the same rules as other adjectives, but **marrón** only has the one singular form and the one plural form.

NB: **naranja** and **violeta** are really nouns, so in this adjectival use they are invariable, i.e. they don't change for masculine/feminine and plurals.

I Complete the sentences with the right form of the colour given in brackets.

a Marta lleva una falda ____(rojo)
b Sus sombreros son ____ (marrón)
c El médico lleva una camisa ____ (verde)
d Su impermeable es ____ (azul)
e María lleva un vestido ____ (naranja)
f Sus zapatos son ____ (blanco)
g Carlos lleva un jersey ____ (violeta)
h Sus sandalias son ____ (amarillo)
i Javier lleva un cinturón ____ (negro)

j Sus botas son ____ (gris)
k Su bufanda es ____ (rosado)

4.1.7 Apocopation

Some adjectives shorten when they come before a noun. This is called **apocopation**. **Bueno**, **malo**, **primero**, **tercero**, **alguno**, **ninguno**, **ciento** and **Santo** change in the masculine singular only. When they are used after a noun they keep their usual form, but if they are used before a masculine singular noun (see 4.2 below) they lose their final **-o**, and **ciento** and **Santo** lose the **t** before it as well. **Grande** becomes **gran** before any singular noun (masculine or feminine).

Hace buen tiempo.	It's good weather.
Un mal día.	A bad day.
El primer presidente de la república.	The first president of the republic.
El tercer hombre en la cola.	The third man in the queue.
No hay ningún chico aquí.	There are no boys here.
El Gran Premio de España.	The Spanish Grand Prix ('big prize').
Tiene cien mil euros.	He has 100,000 euros.
San Sebastián, San José.	San Sebastián, San José.

(But **Santo Domingo**, **Santo Tomás** – male saints' names beginning with **Do-** and **To-** – do not apocopate, to avoid confusion.)

NB: **alguno** and **ninguno** (see 2.7.4) need an accent on the **-u-** in the apocopated form.

I Complete the sentences with the right form of the adjective given in brackets.

a Hace ____ tiempo. (malo)
b El ____ piso a la derecha. (primero)
c Vive en ____ José, en los Estados Unidos. (Santo)
d El Maybach es un ____ coche. (grande)
e La Madre Teresa era una ____ mujer. (grande)
f No hay ____ chica aquí. (ninguno)
g ¡Haces un ____ café! (bueno)
h Tengo ____ euros. (ciento)
i El ____ coche es el Mercedes de la Mafia. (tercero)
j ¿Tienes ____ dinero? (alguno)

4.2 The position of adjectives

In English, adjectives come in front of the noun they are describing: *a large house, a fast car.* In Spanish, most adjectives come after the noun (*a house large, a car fast*). A few adjectives can come before the noun, particularly the ones which apocopate as described in 4.1.7 above.

There are a few adjectives which change their meaning according to whether they come before or after the noun:

una vieja amiga	an old friend (i.e. someone you have known for ages!)
una amiga vieja	an old friend (i.e. someone who isn't young any more!)
un pobre hombre	a poor man (i.e. someone something bad has happened to!)
un hombre pobre	a poor man (i.e. someone who hasn't got very much money!)
El Rey don Carlos es un gran hombre.	King Carlos is a great man.
El Rey don Carlos es un hombre grande.	King Carlos is a large man.

4.3 ▶**Fast track:** Adjectives

Agreement

1 Adjectives are describing words. They agree with the noun they describe, i.e. they usually end in **-o** for masculine nouns, **-a** for feminine nouns, **-os** for masculine plural nouns and **-as** for feminine plural nouns.
2 Adjectives ending in **-e** have the same form for both masculine and feminine singular, and add **-s** (for both masculine and feminine) in the plural.
3 If an adjective ends in a consonant, it again doesn't change in the singular, but it adds **-es** for both masculine and feminine plural.
4 If an adjective ends in **-ete** or **-ote**, the **-e** becomes **-a** in the feminine singular; and **-s** is added to both of these to make the plural forms.
5 If an adjective ends in **-a**, both singular forms are the same and **-s** is added to make the plural.
6 Adjectives ending in **-án**, **-ín**, **-ón** or **-or** have a separate feminine form ending in **-a**, and different plural forms for masculine (**-es**) and feminine (**-as**).
7 Adjectives of nationality or regional origin ending in **-o** or a consonant have feminine singular in **-a**, masculine

plurals in **-os** and **-es** as appropriate, feminine plurals in **-as**; any accent on the masculine singular is not needed on the other forms. Nationalities ending in **-a** and **-e** don't change in the singular, but add **-s** in the plural; the few ending in **-í** add **-es** for the plural.

singular		plural	
masculine	feminine	masculine	feminine
1 un jersey rojo	una camisa roja	jerseys rojos	camisas rojas
2 un coche verde	una moto verde	coches verdes	motos verdes
un hombre fuerte	una mujer fuerte	hombres fuertes	mujeres fuertes
3 un libro azul	una bolsa azul	libros azules	bolsas azules
4 un chico regordete	una chica regordeta	chicos regordetes	chicas regordetas
5 un hombre comunista	una mujer comunista	hombres comunistas	mujeres comunistas
6 un chico holgazán	una chica holgazana	chicos holgazanes	chicas holgazanas
un profesor	una profesora	profesores	profesoras
gruñón	gruñona	gruñones	gruñonas
7 un autor español	una autora española	autores españoles	autoras españolas
un cantante	una cantante	cantantes	cantantas
marroquí	marroquí	marroquíes	marroquíes

Word order

Most adjectives come after the word they are describing:

una mujer guapa	a beautiful woman
un amigo generoso	a generous friend
un edificio moderno	a modern building

... but these often come in front: **bueno**, **malo**, **grande**, **santo**, **alguno**, **ninguno**, **ciento**, **primero**, **tercero** (and other ordinal numbers).

Apocopation

When the adjectives listed above do come in front of masculine nouns, they apocopate, or lose their ending: **ningún dinero**, **cien mil euros**, **el primer piso** but **la primera calle a la derecha**; **grande** apocopates before feminine nouns too: **una gran señora**.

Adjectives with more than one meaning

Some adjectives change their meaning according to whether they come before or after the noun:

| una vieja amiga | an old friend (known her for years!) |
| una amiga vieja | an old friend (getting on a bit!) |

Colours

Like most other adjectives, the adjectives of colour come after the word they are describing: **un perro negro** – *a black dog*. Most colours take the same endings as other adjectives: **amarillo**, **amarilla**, **amarillos**, **amarillas**.

4.4 Big, bigger, biggest: the comparative and superlative

The **comparative** is the form you use when you are comparing two things and say, for example, that something is *bigger, smaller, newer, older*, etc.

The **superlative** is the form you use to say something is the *best, biggest, smallest, best of all*.

adjective	comparative	superlative
big	bigger	biggest
un coche grande	un coche más grande	el coche más grande
small	smaller	smallest
un coche pequeño	un coche más pequeño	el coche más pequeño

 As **grande** and **pequeño** are adjectives, they still have to agree with the noun they describe: **una casa más pequeña** – *a smaller house*; **la casa más pequeña** – *the smallest house*.

4.4.1 Comparing two people or things

In Spanish, you put **más** (*more*) in front of the adjective, and where one thing is compared directly with another, **que** is used for *than*. A handful of adjectives have one-word comparative forms (see 4.4.4).

El Señor García es importante, pero el Señor Pérez es más importante.

Señor García is important but Señor Pérez is more important.

Luis es pequeño, pero su hermana es más pequeña.

Luis is small but his sister is smaller.

Ricardo es inteligente, pero su hermano es más inteligente que él.

Ricardo is intelligent but his brother is more intelligent than him.

I Say the second things are all more ... than the first.

a Este coche es rápido, pero aquél es ____.

b Tu hermana es guapa, pero mi hermana es ____.

c Nuestros perros son grandes, pero los vuestros son ____.

d Las poesías de Machado son muy interesantes, pero las de Lorca son____.

e El examen de español es difícil, pero el de matemáticas es ____.

f Portugal es un país hermoso, pero España es ____.

g Esta casa es muy cara, pero aquélla es aún ____.

h Mis padres son pobres, pero los tuyos son ____.

i Tú vas a comprar un collar precioso, pero yo voy a comprar uno ____.

j Esta bicicleta es bonita: pero buscamos otra ____ para nuestro hijo.

To say something is *less* ... you use **menos** instead of **más**. Again, **que** is used for *than*.

Alejandro es menos viejo que   Alejandro is less old (younger)
   su hermano.   than his brother.

II Say these things are more (+) or less (−).

a (+) El Ferrari es ____ rápido que el Mclaren.

b (+) Un Mercedes es ____ caro que un Seat.

c (−) Nicolás es ____ inteligente que su hermana.

d (+) La culebra (snake) es ____ peligrosa que el alacrán (scorpion).

e (−) El lince es ____ grande que el lobo.

f (+) La Sierra Nevada es ____ alta que la Sierra de Guadarrama.

g (−) La isla de la Gomera es ____ pequeña que la isla de Tenerife.

h (+) Santander se encuentra ____ al norte que Salamanca.

i (−) La plata es ____ valiosa que el oro.

j (+) El Rey don Juan Carlos es ____ famoso que el Presidente del Gobierno.

4.4.2 The superlative: 'the most ...' and 'the least ...'

To say *the most* and *the least* you use **más** and **menos**; if these don't have the noun described immediately in front of them, they are preceded by the definite article that matches the noun. The adjective has to agree with the noun in gender and number, as usual.

el/la/los/las ... más ...
el/la/los/las ... menos ...

La casa más pequeña/Esta casa es la más pequeña.
El perro menos caro/Este perro es el menos caro.
Las niñas más listas/Estas niñas son las más listas.
Los chicos menos tontos/Estos chicos son los menos tontos.

I Say these animals are the most (+).

a (+) El oso pardo es el animal ____ raro que existe en España.

b (+) El alacrán es el bicho ____ peligroso de España.

c (+) La ballena (whale) es el mamífero ____ grande de todos los mamíferos.

d (+) De todos los insectos, el mosquito es ____ peligroso porque lleva la malaria.

e (+) De todos los animales, las jirafas son ____ altas del mundo.

f (+) Las serpientes ____ venenosas se encuentran en Australia.

g (+) De todas las arañas, ____ venenosa se llama la viuda negra.

h (+) Las medusas (jellyfish) más grandes son ____ mortíferas.

II And in Spain: complete these sentences with 'the most' (+) and the correct form of the adjective.

a La montaña ____ se llama el Mulhacén. (+ alto)

b El río ____ es el Ebro. (+ largo)

c La región ____ se llama Los Monegros, y está situada al este de Zaragoza (+ seco)

d De todas las regiones, ____ es Galicia, en el noroeste. (+ lluvioso)

e La ciudad ____ es Bilbao, en el País Vasco. (+ industrializado)

f Entre las cuevas de España, ____ se llama la Cueva de Altamira. (+ famoso)

g Las estalagmitas ____ se encuentran en la Cueva de Altamira. (+ interesante)

h El actor español ____ se llama Antonio Banderas. (+ conocido)

i La actriz ____ se llama Penélope Cruz, y trabaja en Hollywood. (+ guapo)

j La ciudad ____ de España es Sagunto: fue fundada hace más de dos mil años. (+ antigua)

4.4.3 Saying 'as (big) as'

If you are comparing two things that are similar, you use the expression **tan (grande) como**: *as (big) as*. As always, the adjectives have to agree with the noun they are describing.

Es tan grande como su padre.   He is as tall as his father.
Es tan raro como su hermano.   He is as strange as his brother.

(Don't forget that *as much/many as* is **tanto(s)/tanta(s) como** and not **tan mucho como**.)

I Say these places are (1) bigger than; (2), smaller than; (3) as big as ... (Remember to make the adjective agree with the noun where necessary.)

a El Hotel Bellavista es ____ el Hotel Meliá. (3)

b La ciudad de Madrid es ____ la ciudad de Barcelona. (1)

c El puerto de Santander es ____ el puerto de Bilbao. (2)

d Los hipermercados *Hipercor* son ____ los hipermercados *Al Campo*. (2)

e La región autonómica de Extremadura es ____ la de Andalucía. (2)

f Las Torres Kio son ____ que el Palacio de la Comunicación. (1)

II Make these things (1) more, (2) less or (3) just as ... as.

a El Pico del Teide es ＿＿ el Mulhacén. (1 alto)
b El río Guadalquivir es ＿＿ el río Ebro. (2 largo)
c El clima de Canarias es ＿＿ que el clima de España. (1 caluroso)
d El panorama de la sierra es ＿＿ el panorama del lago. (3 hermoso)
e La natación es ＿＿ el footing. (1 agotador)

4.4.4 Better, worse, older and younger: irregular comparisons

The words for *better* and *worse* are irregular and do not form their comparative with **más** or **menos**. Similarly, *bigger/older and smaller/younger* are often translated by one-word comparative forms. These four words are the same for masculine and feminine, and add **-es** in the plural.

better	mejor
worse	peor
bigger/older	mayor
smaller/younger	menor

As with the other comparisons, *than* is expressed by **que**, and it is just omitted if there is no follow-up to the comparison (in other words if only one thing is said to be better, worse, etc.)

Juanita es menor que Josefa.
El francés es bueno pero el español es mejor.

Again as with other comparatives, to make the superlative (*best, worst*, etc.) simply put **el/la/los/las** in front of the comparative form (see 4.4.2).

Dicen que el rioja es el mejor   They say rioja is the
　vino de España.   　best wine in Spain.

I How would you say these things are better?

a Este valdepeñas es bueno, pero el rioja que compraste ayer es ＿＿.
b Mi hijo sacó ＿＿ notas este año que el año pasado.
c El café es bueno, pero el chocolate es aún ＿＿ .
d Estas reproducciones son casi ＿＿ que los originales.
e El clima de Venezuela es ＿＿ que el clima de Chile.
f Las playas del Sardinero son ＿＿ que la playa de Langre.

II How would you say these are the best, according to don Pablo?

Según don Pablo ...

a El rioja es ＿＿ vino de Europa.
b Los vinos españoles son ＿＿ de Europa.
c Las cantantes españolas son ＿＿ del mundo.

d La Sierra Nevada es ____ sierra de Europa.
e Iberia es ____ línea aérea de Europa.
f Los cocineros españoles son ____ del mundo.
g Madrid es ____ capital del mundo.
h España es ____ país de Europa.

4.4.5 ▶**Fast track:** Comparative and superlative

The comparative

The comparative is the form you use when you are comparing two things and say, for example, that something is *bigger, smaller, newer, older,* etc.

In English, we can either add *-er* or use the word *more*:

green → *greener* or *more green*
healthy → *healthier* or *more healthy*
tired → *tireder* or *more tired*

In Spanish, there is only one way: you add the word **más** (*more*) or **menos** (*less*):

más verde; más limpio/a; menos cansado/a

As the word is an adjective it still must agree with the noun:

La hierba es más verde ...   The grass is greener ...
Está menos cansada que yo.   She is less tired than I.

The superlative

When you are talking about *the best* or *the worst* you use the superlative.

In Spanish, the superlative is made by inserting **el**, **la, los** or **las** before the **más** or **menos** unless the article is already used in front of the noun:

el/la más verde; el/la más limpio/a, los/las más cansados/as

As the word is an adjective it must still agree with the noun:

El niño más estúpido.
Esta chica es la más inteligente.
Las historias más interesantes.

NB: After a superlative, Spanish uses **de** to express *in*, e.g. *the ...est* **in** *the world.*

Better, worse, older and younger

The words for *better, worse, bigger/older* and *smaller/younger* (**mejor**, **peor**, **mayor** and **menor**) are irregular one-word comparison. They have the same form for masculine and feminine and add **-es** for the plural.

Que is omitted if there is no follow-up to the comparison:

El francés es bueno pero el español es mejor.

The same words are used with the definite article to mean *best, worst, biggest/eldest* and *smallest/youngest.*

5 ADVERBS

What is an adverb?

Adverbs are words which describe the action of a verb: she drives *fast;* he speaks *loudly.*

Some adverbs can qualify an adjective or adverb, e.g. *very* (fast), *quite* (loud), *too* (hard).

5.1 Formation of adverbs

5.1.1 Regular adverbs

Adverbs are words which describe an action: *well, fast, slowly*, etc.

Many Spanish adverbs are formed by adding **-mente** to the feminine singular form of an adjective, if this is different from the masculine singular. If there was an accent on the adjective, it remains on the adverb:

dulce → dulcemente	gently
lento/lenta → lentamente	slowly
rápido/rápida → rápidamente	quickly
feroz/feroz → ferozmente	ferociously

I Make these adjectives into adverbs.

a	seco	**f**	sincero
b	loco	**g**	raro
c	sencillo	**h**	feliz
d	rápido	**i**	verdadero
e	enorme	**j**	serio

5.1.2 Irregular adverbs

bueno/buena → bien	well
malo/mala → mal	badly

5.1.3 Pairs of adverbs

When two adjectives are used together, only the second one has **-mente** on the end. The first one is always in the feminine form, however.

rápida y seguramente	quickly and safely

5.2 Other useful adverbs

The following adverbs are very common, so it is worth learning them:

muy	very
bastante	quite
demasiado	too
poco	little
despacio	slowly

Some adverbs of time:

siempre	always
a veces	sometimes
muchas veces	often

5.3 Comparison of adverbs

The comparative and superlative of adverbs are formed and used in exactly the same way as those of adjectives (see 4.4).

| Felipe trabaja menos rápidamente que su hermana. | Felipe works less quickly than his sister. |
| María corre mas lentamente que su amiga. | Maria runs more slowly than her friend. |

I How would you say the following?

a Speak more slowly, please!   ¡Habla más ____ , por favor!
b He is completely mad.   Está ____ loco.
c That's not strictly true!   ¡No es ____ la verdad!
d It's too expensive.   Es ____ caro.
e Speak more loudly, please.   Hable más ____ por favor.

5.4 ▶Fast track: Adverbs

In English, most words which end in *-ly* are adverbs: *naturally, romantically, sadly*, etc.

In Spanish, many adverbs are made by adding **-mente** to the feminine singular form of an adjective, if it is different from the masculine:

dulce → dulcemente
seguro/segura → seguramente
regular → regularmente

If there was an accent on the original adjective, it remains:

rápido/rápida → rápidamente

Some useful adverbs:

bien	well
mal	badly
poco	little
mejor	better
fuerte	loudly/strongly
siempre	always
a veces	sometimes
muchas veces	frequently/often

These words are often used with another adverb or adjective:

muy	very	muy pequeño	very small
		muy guapo	very beautiful
bastante	quite	bastante feo	quite ugly
poco	not very	poco hermoso	not very beautiful
demasiado	too	demasiado caro	too expensive

6 PREPOSITIONS

6.1 Recognising prepositions

▶▶ **If you know what a preposition is, go on to 6.2.**

Prepositions are words like *in, on,* and *under.* Unlike adjectives, they do not change. They are usually used in conjunction with a noun or pronoun, e.g. *in the cupboard, near the station, for her, with me.*

Prepositions can tell you:

- **where** a person or thing is, i.e. its position:
sobre la mesa	on the table
debajo del puente	under the bridge

- **how** something is, i.e. manner:
con mantequilla	with butter
sin agua	without water

- **when** something happens, i.e. time:
dentro de cinco minutos	in five minutes
después de la cena	after dinner

- **for whom** something is done:
para mí	for me

6.2 Using prepositions

6.2.1 *a* and *en*

The principal usage of **a** is to translate *to,* although sometimes it can mean *at* or *in.* It usually indicates motion to a place. Note that **a** combines with **el** to become **al** – *to the* with masculine singular nouns.

Escribo a mi amigo.	I am writing *to* my friend.
Volvemos a casa.	We are going (*to*) home.
Vamos al pueblo.	We are going *to the* town.
El tren llega a Barcelona a las dos.	The train arrives *at/in* Barcelona *at* two o'clock.

En is usually used to show something's position *at* or *in* a place or thing:

Estamos en casa.	We are *at* home.
El tren está en la estación.	The train is *in* the station.
Vivo en Madrid.	I live *in* Madrid.

6.2.2 *por* and *para*

The meaning of **para** is usually *for, in order to*, expressing destination and intention; the main meaning of **por** is usually translated as *by, through* or *because of* – but occasionally it can also mean *for*.

¿Es para ti?	Is it for you?
Para mí un helado, por favor.	For me an ice-cream, please.
Estoy citado para las ocho.	I have an appointment for eight o'clock.
Pasamos por Madrid.	We passed through Madrid.
No podemos ver por los árboles.	We can't see for (because of) the trees.
Lo hago por ti.	I am doing it for you (for your sake).

6.2.3 *con* and *sin*

The meaning of **con** is usually *with*, and the main meaning of **sin** is usually translated as *without*. **Sin** is usually used without the definite article. When **con** is used with certain personal pronouns it changes to the special forms **conmigo**, **contigo**, **consigo** (see 3.4).

Patatas fritas con salsa de tomate, por favor.	Chips with tomato sauce please.
Mi madre viene conmigo.	My mother is coming with me.
Una botella de agua mineral sin gas, por favor.	A bottle of mineral water without gas, please.

6.2.4 *de* and *entre*

The meaning of **de** is usually *of*, but it can also mean *from* or *for* according to the context. Note that **de** combines with **el** to become **del** – *from the* with masculine singular nouns. **De** also figures in **expressions** of belonging and saying what something is made of. **Entre** means *between* or *among*.

Vengo de Madrid.	I have come from Madrid.
Bebo una taza de té.	I am drinking a cup of tea.
but Compro una taza de té.	I buy a teacup (= cup *for* tea).
Es la casa de mi amigo.	It is my friend's house.
Quiero un helado de vainilla.	I want a vanilla ice-cream.
Entre los árboles.	Among the trees.

| Entre las casas. | Between the houses. | **175** |
| Entre nosotros. | Between/Among us. | |

6.2.5 *hacia* and *hasta*

The meaning of **hacia** is usually *towards*, and **hasta** usually translates *until*, *up to* or *as far as*.

Hacia el tejado.	Towards the roof.
Hacia la cima.	Towards the top.
Hasta mañana.	Until tomorrow.
Hasta luego.	Until then (i.e. 'see you later')

6.2.6 *según*

The meaning of **según** is *according to (what)*. It corresponds to *selon* in French. By itself it means *it depends*.

Según mi madre.	According to my mother.
Según piensa.	According to what he thinks.
¿Vienes conmigo? Según.	Are you coming with me? It depends.

6.2.7 *sobre, en* and *encima de*

Sobre and **en** both mean *on*, and can be used with either horizontal or vertical surfaces. **Encima de** (and sometimes **sobre**) means *on top of*, and **encima de** can also mean *above*.

Está en la pared.	It is on the wall.
Está sobre la silla.	It is on the chair.
Está encima de la mesa.	It's on (top of) the table.
Encima de la ventana.	Above the window.

6.2.8 *detrás de, tras* and *después de*

The meaning of **detrás de** is *behind*. **Tras** has the same meaning and can also mean *after* or *as a result of*. **Después de** means *after*.

| Detrás de la tienda. | Behind the shop. |
| Después del/Tras el programa. | After the programme. |

6.2.9 *delante de, ante* and *enfrente de*

Delante de and **ante** mean *in front of*. **Ante** can also mean *faced with* or *in the presence of*. **Enfrente de** means *opposite*.

6.2.10 *desde*

Desde means *from* (a place) and is also used for *since* in time expressions. (For **desde hace** see 1.8.10.)

| La vista desde el balcón es espectacular. | The view from the balcony is spectacular. |
| Vivo aquí desde abril. | I've been living here since April. |

I How would you say you were going to these places? Take care with **al** ...

Voy ...

a la playa

b el hotel

c la piscina

d el hospital

e el museo

f la discoteca

g el teatro

h la estación de servicio

i el banco

j el cajero automático (cashpoint)

II Say what these things are made of or who they belong to. Take care with **del** ...

a un bocadillo ____ jamón   a ham sandwich

b un helado ____ chocolate   a chocolate ice-cream

c los libros ____ chicas   the girls' books

d el coche ____ profesor   the teacher's car

e el maletero ____ coche   the boot of the car

f una taza ____ café   a cup of coffee

g una botella ____ vino tinto   a bottle of red wine

h el jardín ____ amigos   the friends' garden

i la carta ____ mi madre   my mother's letter

j una tortilla ____ patatas   a potato omelette

III Complete these sentences with the correct preposition(s). Take care with **a** and **de** if followed by **el**.

a Anoche fui ____ pueblo ____ mi amigo.   Last night I went to town with my friend.

b Pasamos un par de horas ____ el bar.   We spent a couple of hours in the bar.

c Allí, charlamos ____ dos chicas guapas.   There we chatted to two pretty girls.

d Después, fuimos ____ cafetería.   Then we went to the cafeteria.

e La cafetería está ____ bar.   The cafeteria is opposite the bar.

f ____ cenar, fuimos ____ discoteca.   After having dinner, we went to the disco.

g Las dos chicas bailaron ____ nosotros.   The two girls danced with us.

h Nos quedamos ____ medianoche.   We stayed until midnight.

6.2.10 ▶Fast track: Prepositions

Prepositions are words like *in, on* and *under*. They do not change. They tell you:

- **where** a person or thing is, i.e. its position
- **how** something is done, i.e. manner

- **when** something happens, i.e. time
- **for whom** something is done

etc.

a and en

A expresses movement: it usually means *to*, occasionally *at* or *in*. **En** means *at* or *in*, indicating position.

por and para

Para means *for, in order to*, expressing destination and intention; **por** usually means *for, by, through* or *because of*.

con and sin

The meaning of **con** is usually *with*, and **sin** is usually translated as *without*.

de and entre

The meaning of **de** is usually *of, from* or *for*, and it is used to express ownership and what something is made of. **Entre** means *between* or *among*.

hacia and hasta

Hacia usually means *towards*, and **hasta** is usually *until, up to* or *as far as*.

según

The meaning of **según** is *according to (what)*. By itself it means *it depends*.

sobre, en and encima de

Sobre and **en** mean *on*. **Encima de**, and sometimes **sobre**, mean *on top of* or *above*.

detrás de, tras and después de

Detrás de means *behind*. **Tras** can mean *behind, after* or *as a result of*. **Después de** means *after*.

delante de, enfrente de and ante

Delante de and **ante** mean *in front of*. **Ante** can mean *faced with* or *in the presence of*. **Enfrente de** means *opposite*.

desde

Desde usually means *from* or *since*.

AND OTHER USEFUL WORDS

Here are some useful words for joining two parts of a sentence or filling in gaps in a conversation. These are often called connectives.

y	and
o	or
pero	but
porque	because
entonces	then
por tanto	then, so
en todo caso	anyway
pues bien ...	well then ...
aquí lo tiene	here it is
¡caramba!	oh dear!
es todo	that's all

- When **y** is followed by a word beginning with **i-** or **hi-** it changes to **e**.
- When **o** is followed by a word beginning with **o-** or **ho-** it changes to **u**.

VERB TABLES

This chapter lists regular verb forms and the main irregular verb forms for the tenses covered in this book. For those who wish to take their studies further, the present subjunctive and imperfect subjunctive tenses have been included.

Emboldened verb forms indicate a stem-change from the infinitive.

Regular verbs

Infinitive	Present indicative	Present subjunctive	Imperative	Future	Conditional	Imperfect indicative	Preterite	Imperfect subjunctive	Gerund / Past participle
-ar verbs **pasar** to pass, spend (time), happen	paso	pase		pasaré	pasaría	pasaba	pasé	pasara / pasase	pasando
	pasas	pases	pasa (tú)	pasarás	pasarías	pasabas	pasaste	pasaras / pasases	
	pasa	pase	pase Vd	pasará	pasaría	pasaba	pasó	pasara / pasase	pasado
	pasamos	pasemos		pasaremos	pasaríamos	pasábamos	pasamos	pasáramos / pasásemos	
	pasáis	paséis	pasad (vosotros)	pasaréis	pasaríais	pasabais	pasasteis	pasarais / pasaseis	
	pasan	pasen	pasen Vds	pasarán	pasarían	pasaban	pasaron	pasaran / pasasen	
-er verbs **beber** to drink	bebo	beba		beberé	bebería	bebía	bebí	bebiera / bebiese	bebiendo
	bebes	bebas	bebe (tú)	beberás	beberás	bebías	bebías	bebiera / bebiese	bebiera /
	bebe	beba	beba Vd	beberá	bebería	bebía	bebió	bebiera / bebiese	
	beb**emos***	bebamos		beberemos	beberíamos	bebíamos	bebimos	bebiéramos / bebiésemos	bebido
	beb**éis***	bebáis	beb**ed*** (vosotros)	beberéis	beberíais	bebíais	bebisteis	bebierais / bebieseis	
	beben	beban	beban Vds	beberán	beberían	bebían	bebieron	bebieran /	

-ir verbs
subir
to go up, come up

	Present	Present subjunctive	Imperative	Future	Conditional	Imperfect	Preterite	Imperfect subjunctive	
	subo	suba		subiré	subiría	subía	subí	subiera / subiese	subiendo
	subes	subas	sube (tú)	subirás	subirías	subías	subiste	subieras / subieses	
	sube	suba	suba Vd	subirá	subiría	subía	subió	subiera / subiese	
	sub**imos***	subamos		subiremos	subiríamos	subíamos	subimos	subiéramos / subiésemos	subido
	sub**ís***	subáis	sub**id*** (vosotros)	subiréis	subiríais	subías	subisteis	subierais / subieseis	
	suben	suban	suban Vds	subirán	subirían	subían	subieron	subieran / subiesen	

*These are the only three places where regular **-er** and **-ir** verbs have different endings

The main irregular verbs

Infinitive	Present indicative	Present subjunctive	Imperative	Future	Conditional	Imperfect indicative	Preterite	Imperfect subjunctive	Gerund / Past participle
caber to fit, be contained	**quepo**	**quepa**		cabré	cabría	cabía	cupe	cupiera / cupiese	cabiendo
	cabes	**quepas**	cabe	cabrás	cabrías	cabías	cupiste	cupieras / cupieses	
	cabes	**quepa**	**quepa** Vd	cabrá	cabría	cabía	cupo	cupiera / cupiese	cabido
	cabemos	**quepamos**		cabremos	cabríamos	cabíamos	cupimos	cupiéramos / cupiésemos	
	cabéis	**quepáis**	cabed	cabréis	cabríais	cabíais	cupisteis	cupierais / cupieseis	
	caben	**quepan**	**quepan** Vds	cabrán	cabrían	cabían	cupieron	cupieran / cupiesen	
caer to fall	**caigo**	**caiga**		caeré	caería	caía	caí	cayera / cayese	cayendo
	caes	**caigas**	cae	caerás	caerías	caías	caíste	cayeras / cayeses	
	cae	**caiga**	**caiga** Vd	caerá	caería	caía	cayó	cayera / cayese	caído
	caemos	**caigamos**		caeremos	caeríamos	caíamos	caímos	cayéramos / cayésemos	
	caéis	**caigáis**	caed	caeréis	caeríais	caíais	caísteis	cayerais / cayeseis	

	Present	Present subjunctive	Imperative	Future	Conditional	Imperfect	Preterite	Imperfect subjunctive	Gerund / Past participle
(caer)	caen	caigan	caigan Vds	caerán	caerían	caían	cayeron	cayeran / cayesen	conduciendo
conducir to drive, lead and all other verbs ending in **-ducir**	conduzco conduces conduce conducimos conducís conducen	conduzca conduzcas conduzca conduzcamos conduzcáis conduzcan	conduce conduzca Vd conducid conduzcan Vds	conduciré conducirás conducirá conduciremos conduciréis conducirán	conduciría conducirías conduciría conduciríamos conduciríais conducirían	conducía conducías conducía conducíamos conducíais conducían	conduje condujiste condujo condujimos condujisteis condujeron	condujera / condujese condujeras / condujeses condujera / condujese condujéramos / condujésemos condujerais / condujeseis condujeran / condujesen	conducido
dar to give	doy das da damos dais dan	dé des dé demos deis den	da dé Vd dad den Vds	daré darás dará daremos daréis darán	daría darías daría daríamos daríais darían	daba dabas daba dábamos dabais daban	di diste dio dimos disteis dieron	diera / diese dieras / dieses diera / diese diéramos / diésemos dierais / dieseis dieran / diesen	dando dado
decir to say, tell	digo dices dice decimos	diga digas diga digamos	di diga Vd	diré dirás dirá diremos	diría dirías diría diríamos	decía decías decía decíamos	dije dijiste dijo dijimos	dijera / dijese dijeras / dijeses dijera / dijese dijéramos / dijésemos	diciendo dicho

Verb Tables

Infinitive	Present indicative	Present subjunctive	Imperative	Future	Conditional	Imperfect indicative	Preterite	Imperfect subjunctive	Gerund / Past participle
	decís	digáis	decid	diréis	diríais	decíais	dijisteis	dijerais / dijeseis	
	dicen	digan	digan Vds	dirán	dirían	decían	dijeron	dijeran / dijesen	
estar to be	estoy	esté		estaré	estaría	estaba	estuve	estuviera / estuviese	estando
	estás	estés	está	estarás	estarías	estabas	estuviste	estuvieras / estuvieses	
	está	esté	esté Vd	estará	estaría	estaba	estuvo	estuviera / estuviese	
	estamos	estemos		estaremos	estaríamos	estábamos	estuvimos	estuviéramos / estuviésemos	estado
	estáis	estéis	estad	estaréis	estaríais	estabais	estuvisteis	estuvierais / estuvieseis	
	están	estén	estén Vds	estarán	estarían	estaban	estuvieron	estuvieran / estuviesen	
haber to have (as auxiliary verb only) hay = there is/are	he	haya		habré	habría	había	hube	hubiera / hubiese	habiendo
	has	hayas		habrás	habrías	habías	hubiste	hubieras / hubieses	
	ha (hay)	haya		habrá	habría	había	hubo	hubiera / hubiese	
	hemos	hayamos		habremos	habríamos	habíamos	hubimos	hubiéramos / hubiésemos	habido

haber (continued)

	Present	Present subj.	Imperative	Future	Conditional	Imperfect	Preterite	Imperfect subjunctive	Gerund/Participle
	habéis	hayáis		habréis	habriais	habiais	hubisteis	hubierais / hubieseis	
	han	hayan		habrán	habrían	habían	hubieron	hubieran / hubiesen	

hacer — to do, make

	Present	Present subj.	Imperative	Future	Conditional	Imperfect	Preterite	Imperfect subjunctive	Gerund/Participle
	hago	haga		haré	haría	hacía	hice	hiciera / hiciese	haciendo
	haces	hagas	haz	harás	harías	hacías	hiciste	hicieras / hicieses	
	hace	haga	haga Vd	hará	haría	hacía	hizo	hiciera / hiciese	hecho
	hacemos	hagamos		haremos	haríamos	hacíamos	hicimos	hiciéramos / hiciésemos	
	hacéis	hagáis	haced	haréis	haríais	hacíais	hicisteis	hicierais / hicieseis	
	hacen	hagan	hagan Vds	harán	harían	hacían	hicieron	hicieran / hiciesen	

ir — to go

	Present	Present subj.	Imperative	Future	Conditional	Imperfect	Preterite	Imperfect subjunctive	Gerund/Participle
	voy	vaya		iré	iría	iba	fui	fuera / fuese	yendo
	vas	vayas	ve	irás	irías	ibas	fuiste	fueras / fueses	
	va	vaya	vaya Vd	irá	iría	iba	fue	fuera / fuese	
	vamos	vayamos		iremos	iríamos	íbamos	fuimos	fuéramos / fuésemos	ido
	vais	vayáis	id	iréis	iríais	ibais	fuisteis	fuerais / fueseis	
	van	vayan	vayan Vds	irán	irían	iban	fueron	fueran / fuesen	

oír — to hear

	Present	Present subj.	Imperative	Future	Conditional	Imperfect	Preterite	Imperfect subjunctive	Gerund/Participle
	oigo	oiga		oiré	oiría	oía	oí	oyera / oyese	oyendo
	oyes	oigas	oye	oirás	oirías	oías	oíste	oyeras / oyeses	

Infinitive	Present indicative	Present subjunctive	Imperative	Future	Conditional	Imperfect indicative	Preterite	Imperfect subjunctive	Gerund / Past participle
	oye	**oiga**		oirá	oiría	oía	**oyó**	**oyera / oyese**	
	oímos	**oigamos**	**oiga** Vd	oiremos	oiríamos	oíamos	oímos	**oyéramos / oyésemos**	
	ós	**oigáis**	oíd	oiréis	oiríais	oíais	oísteis	**oyerais / oyeseis**	oído
	oyen	**oigan**	**oigan** Vds	oirán	oirían	oían	**oyeron**	**oyeran / oyesen**	
poder to be able, can	**puedo**	**pueda**		**podré**	**podría**	podía	**pude**	**pudiera / pudiese**	**pudiendo**
	puedes	**puedas**		**podrás**	**podrías**	podías	**pudiste**	**pudieras / pudieses**	
	puede	**pueda**		**podrá**	**podría**	podía	**pudo**	**pudiera / pudiese**	podido
	podemos	podamos		**podremos**	**podríamos**	podíamos	**pudimos**	**pudiéramos / pudiésemos**	
	podéis	podáis		**podréis**	**podrías**	podíais	**pudisteis**	**pudierais / pudieseis**	
	pueden	**puedan**		**podrán**	**podrían**	podían	**pudieron**	**pudieran / pudiesen**	
poner to put	**pongo**	**ponga**		**pondré**	**pondría**	ponía	**puse**	**pusiera / pusiese**	poniendo
	pones	**pongas**	**pon**	**pondrás**	**pondrías**	ponías	**pusiste**	**pusieras / pusieses**	
	pone	**ponga**	**ponga** Vd	**pondrá**	**pondría**	ponía	**puso**	**pusiera / pusiese**	

poner (continued)

Present	Present subj.	Imperative	Future	Conditional	Imperfect	Preterite	Imperfect subj.	Participle
ponemos	pongamos		pondremos	pondríamos	poníamos	pusimos	pusiéramos / pusiésemos	puesto
ponéis	pongáis	poned	pondréis	pondríais	poníais	pusisteis	pusierais / pusieseis	
ponen	pongan	pongan Vds	pondrán	pondrían	ponían	pusieron	pusieran / pusiesen	

querer to want, love

Present	Present subj.	Imperative	Future	Conditional	Imperfect	Preterite	Imperfect subj.	Participle
quiero	quiera		querré	querría	quería	quise	quisiera / quisiese	queriendo
quieres	quieras	quiere	querrás	querrías	querías	quisiste	quisieras / quisieses	
quiere	quiera	quiera Vd	querrá	querría	quería	quiso	quisiera / quisiese	querido
queremos	queramos		querremos	querríamos	queríamos	quisimos	quisiéramos / quisiésemos	
queréis	queráis	quered	querréis	querríais	queríais	quisisteis	quisierais / quisieseis	
quieren	quieran	quieran Vds	querrán	querrían	querían	quisieron	quisieran / quisiesen	

saber to know

Present	Present subj.	Imperative	Future	Conditional	Imperfect	Preterite	Imperfect subj.	Participle
sé	sepa		sabré	sabría	sabía	supe	supiera / supiese	sabiendo
sabes	sepas	sabe	sabrás	sabrías	sabías	supiste	supieras / supieses	
sabe	sepa	sepa Vd	sabrá	sabría	sabía	supo	supiera / supiese	sabido
sabemos	sepamos		sabremos	sabríamos	sabíamos	supimos	supiéramos / supiésemos	
sabéis	sepáis	sabed	sabréis	sabríais	sabíais	supisteis	supierais / supieseis	

[handwritten top margin: Subjunctive: a wish for something to be true / expres something contrary to what is true]

[handwritten left margin: Indicative: fact, opinion, assertion, question. Imperative: command. Subjunctive]

[handwritten corner: MCD]

Verb Tables

Infinitive	Present indicative	Present subjunctive	Imperative	Future	Conditional indicative	Imperfect *(past 'used to' / continuous)*	Preterite *(completed past action)*	Imperfect subjunctive	Gerund / Past participle
	saben	sepan	sepan Vds	sabrán	sabrán	sabían	supieron	supieran / supiesen	
salir to go out, come out	salgo	salga		saldré	saldría	salía	salí	saliera / saliese	saliendo
	sales	salgas	sal	saldrás	saldrías	salías	saliste	salieras / salieses	
	sale	salga	salga Vd	saldrá	saldría	salía	salió	saliera / saliese	salido
	salimos	salgamos		saldremos	saldríamos	salíamos	salimos	saliéramos / saliésemos	
	salís	salgáis	salid	saldréis	saldríais	salíais	salisteis	salierais / salieseis	
	salen	salgan	salgan Vds	saldrán	saldrían	salían	salieron	salieran / saliesen	
ser to be	soy	sea	sé	seré	sería	era	fui	fuera / fuese	siendo
	eres	seas	sea Vd	serás	serías	eras	fuiste	fueras / fueses	
	es	sea		será	sería	era	fue	fuera / fuese	sido
	somos	seamos		seremos	seríamos	éramos	fuimos	fuéramos / fuésemos	
	sois	seáis	sed	seréis	seríais	erais	fuisteis	fuerais / fueseis	
	son	sean	sean Vds	serán	serían	eran	fueron	fueran / fuesen	
tener to have	tengo	tenga	ten	tendré	tendría	tenía	tuve	tuviera / tuviese	teniendo
	tienes	tengas	tenga Vd	tendrás	tendrías	tenías	tuviste	tuvieras / tuvieses	
	tiene	tenga		tendrá	tendría	tenía	tuvo	tuviera / tuviese	

	Present indicative	Present subjunctive	Imperative	Future	Conditional	Imperfect	Preterite	Imperfect subjunctive	Gerund / Past participle
	tenemos	tengamos		tendremos	tendríamos	teníamos	tuvimos	tuviéramos / tuviésemos	
	tenéis	tengáis	tened	tendréis	tendríais	teníais	tuvisteis	tuvierais / tuvieseis	
	tienen	tengan	tengan Vds	tendrán	tendrían	tenían	tuvieron	tuvieran / tuviesen	tenido
traer to bring	**traigo**	**traiga**		traeré	traería	traía	**traje**	**trajera / trajese**	**trayendo**
	traes	**traigas**	trae	traerás	traerías	traías	**trajiste**	**trajeras / trajeses**	
	trae	**traiga**	**traiga** Vd	traerá	traería	traía	**trajo**	**trajera / trajese**	traído
	traemos	**traigamos**		traeremos	traeríamos	traíamos	**trajimos**	**trajéramos / trajésemos**	
	traéis	**traigáis**	traed	traeréis	traeríais	traíais	**trajisteis**	**trajerais / trajeseis**	
	traen	**traigan**	**traigan** Vds	traerán	traerían	traían	**trajeron**	**trajeran / trajesen**	
venir to come	**vengo**	**venga**		**vendré**	**vendría**	venía	**vine**	**viniera / viniese**	**viniendo**
	vienes	**vengas**	**ven**	**vendrás**	**vendrías**	venías	**viniste**	**vinieras / vinieses**	
	viene	**venga**	**venga** Vd	**vendrá**	**vendría**	venía	**vino**	**viniera / viniese**	venido
	venimos	**vengamos**		**vendremos**	**vendríamos**	veníamos	**vinimos**	**viniéramos / viniésemos**	
	venís	**vengáis**	venid	**vendréis**	**vendríais**	veníais	**vinisteis**	**vinierais / vinieseis**	
	vienen	**vengan**	**vengan** Vds	**vendrán**	**vendrían**	venían	**vinieron**	**vinieran / viniesen**	

Verb Tables

Note also:

- **andar** has a 'Pretérito grave' (**anduve**, etc.) and therefore the imperfect subjunctive is **anduviera/anduviese**, etc.
- **ver** has **veo, ves**, etc. in present indicative, **vea**, etc. in present subjunctive and **veía**, etc. in imperfect indicative.
- **abrir, cubrir, descubrir, freír, romper** and **volver** have irregular past participles – see 1.4.2.

1.1

I a, c, d, i

II b, c, f, h, i

1.1.1

I **a** to speak **b** to prepare **c** to organise **d** to enter **e** to travel **f** to carry/wear **g** to look at/check **h** to invite **i** to wash **j** to study

II **a** to cook **b** to dine **c** to have breakfast **d** to appreciate **e** to roast **f** to have a teatime snack **g** to pour **h** to cut **i** to have to eat or drink **j** to lunch **k** to mix

III **a** comenzar **b** aceptar **c** separar **d** evaluar **e** robar **f** navegar **g** publicar **h** girar **i** continuar **j** terminar

1.1.2

I **a** 2 vend **b** 1 mostr **c** 1 cant **d** 3 sal **e** 1 lav **f** 1 acab **g** 1 escuch **h** 1 cerr **i** 1 dej **j** 2 cog **k** 2 escog **l** 1 llev **m** 1 regres **n** 3 ven **o** 3 dorm

1.1.3

I **a** saber **b** ver **c** tener **d** ir **e** poder **f** deber **g** querer **h** coger **i** ser **j** hacer

1.1.4

I **a** yo **b** ella **c** él **d** nosotros **e** vosotras **f** usted **g** ellas **h** ellos

II **a** él **b** ella **c** él **d** ellos **e** ellas **f** ellas **g** yo **h** ellos **i** ellos **j** nosotros

1.2

I **a** descargar – to download **b** telefonear – to telephone **c** acompañar – to accompany **d** ir – to go **e** (ir a) recoger – to fetch **f** prestar – to lend **g** volar – to fly **h** visitar – to visit **i** estudiar – to study **j** cenar – to dine

1.2.1

I **a** I am singing **b** you are eating (familiar sing.) **c** he/she/it is drinking, you (formal) are drinking **d** we are working **e** you are travelling (familiar pl.) **f** they/you (formal) are going up

1.2.2

I **a** hablo **b** tomo **c** llevo **d** trabajo **e** escucho **f** toco **g** visito **h** miro **i** llego **j** explico

II **a** trabajo **b** llego **c** aparco **d** entro **e** saludo **f** tomo **g** busco **h** entro **i** saco **j** trabajo

III **a** entro **b** compro **c** llamo
d tomo **e** pago **f** envío
g espero **h** trato **i** echo
j felicito

IV **a** hablo **b** viajo **c** quedo
d llamo **e** llego **f** entro
g compro **h** espero **i** ceno
j mando **k** charlo **l** tomo
m telefoneo **n** miro

V **a** beber **b** comer **c** correr
d responder **e** vender **f** leer
g comprender **h** proceder
i aprender **j** creer

VI **a** bebo **b** como **c** corro
d leo **e** vendo **f** aprendo
g procedo **h** creo **i** comprendo
j respondo

VII **a** vivo **b** subo **c** sufro
d escribo **e** describo **f** divido
g recibo **h** asisto

VIII **a** subo **b** vivo **c** decido
d asisto **e** discuto **f** sufro
g persuado **h** admito **i** divido
j sobrevivo

IX **a** discuto **b** subo **c** descubro
d divido **e** cubro **f** abro

X **a** tengo **b** tengo **c** sé
d pongo **e** salgo **f** conozco
g digo **h** sé **i** doy

XI **a** quiero **b** pienso **c** pido
d cuento **e** juego **f** prefiero
g vuelvo **h** duermo

XII **a** me despierto **b** me levanto
c me lavo **d** me ducho **e** me
visto **f** me siento **g** me pregunto
h me aburro **i** me peleo **j** me
acuesto

XIII **a** me ducle **b** me hace falta
c me quedan **d** me gustan **e** me
apetece **f** me encantan **g** me
interesan

1.2.3

I **a** bailas **b** bebes **c** vives
d hablas **e** miras **f** comes
g escuchas **h** escribes **i** lavas
j trabajas

II **a** quieres **b** piensas **c** pides
d cuentas **e** juegas **f** prefieres
g vuelves **h** duermes

III **a** eres **b** tienes **c** vas
d comes **e** ves **f** vives **g** hablas
h llevas **i** haces **j** juegas

IV **a** ii **b** iv **c** v **d** iii **e** i

V **a** te duelen **b** te hacen falta
c te quedan **d** te gusta **e** te
apetece **f** te encantan **g** te
interesan

VI **a** tienes **b** sales **c** coges
d llegas **e** cenas **f** vuelves

VII **a** iii **b** vi **c** v **d** vii **e** i
f ix **g** iv **h** ii **i** x **j** viii

1.2.4

I **a** escribe **b** canta **c** navega
d lee **e** recibe **f** vende
g desea **h** presta **i** prepara
j firma

II **a** juega **b** piensa **c** pide
d cuenta **e** quiere **f** prefiere
g vuelve **h** duerme

III **a** es **b** vive **c** va **d** coge
e pasa **f** llega **g** tiene **h** pone
i llama **j** vuelve

IV **a** se despierta **b** se levanta
c se afeita **d** se ducha **e** se lava
f se seca **g** se peina **h** se viste
i se sienta **j** se aburre **k** se pasea
l se cansa **m** se acuesta

V **a** lee **b** va **c** toma
d duerme **e** hace **f** toma **g** tiene
h dice

1.2.5

I **a** trabajamos **b** jugamos
c vemos **d** cenamos
e regresamos **f** vamos **g** salimos
h llegamos **i** compramos
j tenemos

II **a** somos **b** hablamos **c** vamos
d escogemos **e** cogemos
f cambiamos **g** comprendemos
h comemos **i** trabajamos
j terminamos **k** jugamos

III Nos + **a** despertamos
b levantamos **c** acostamos
d duchamos **e** damos prisa
f vestimos **g** lavamos **h** paseamos
i separamos

IV **a** tenemos **b** somos
c quedamos **d** comemos
e podemos **f** no venimos **g** no
comprendemos **h** queremos
i vamos **j** vemos **k** salimos
l llegamos **m** venimos **n** hacemos
o leemos

1.2.6

II **a** ¿Os acordáis de este hombre?
b ¿Os paseáis por el parque?
c ¿Os vestís ya? **d** ¿Os burláis de
mí? **e** ¿Os levantáis tarde?
f ¿Os despertáis temprano?

1.2.7

I **a** juegan **b** piensan **c** piden
d encuentran **e** quieren
f prefieren **g** vuelven **h** duermen

II **a** quieren **b** tienen **c** van
d dejan **e** hacen **f** salen
g encuentran **h** buscan **i** ven
j llaman

III **a** se despiertan **b** se levantan
c se duchan **d** se preparan

e salen **f** van **g** llegan **h** se
aburren **i** se van

IV **a** obtienen **b** van **c** pueden
d necesitan **e** tienen **f** deben
g suben **h** viajan

1.2.8

II **a** tengo **b** estoy **c** voy
d cojo **e** bajo **f** salgo **g** cruzo
h espero **i** quiero **j** vuelvo

II **a** tienes **b** estás **c** vas
d coges **e** bajas **f** sales **g** cruzas
h esperas **i** quieres **j** vuelves

III **a** tiene **b** está **c** va **d** coge
e baja **f** sale **g** cruza **h** espera
i quiere **j** vuelve

IV **a** tenemos **b** estamos
c vamos **d** cogemos **e** bajamos
f salimos **g** cruzamos
h esperamos **i** queremos
j volvemos

V **a** tenéis **b** estáis **c** vais
d cogéis **e** bajáis **f** salís
g cruzáis **h** esperáis **i** queréis
j volvéis

VI **a** tienen **b** están **c** van
d cogen **e** bajan **f** salen
g cruzan **h** esperan **i** quieren
j vuelven

1.3.1

I **a** no beben **b** no escribo **c** no
lee **d** no compramos **e** no sé
f no puede **g** no vienen **h** no
quiero **i** no nos gusta
j no comes

1.3.2

I
a ¿Viven los señores Blanco en
Madrid?
b ¿Salen ellos de vacaciones?

c ¿Cogen ellos el tren?
d ¿Van ellos a la Costa del Sol?
e ¿Tienen ellos un apartamento allí?
f ¿Alquilan ellos un coche?
g ¿Juegan ellos al golf?
h ¿Hacen ellos esquí acuático?
i ¿Tienen ellos unos amigos en Fuengirola?
j Por la tarde, ¿cenan ellos en un restaurante?

II   a ¿Adónde van ellos?
b ¿Cuándo salen ellos?   c ¿Cómo viajan ellos?   d ¿Por qué están ellos en Barcelona?   e ¿Qué hacen ellos?   f ¿Con quién tienen ellos una reunión?
g ¿Cuánto tiempo se quedan ellos en el hotel?

1.3.3

I   a cállate b no te sientes   c ten
d dame e sé f no vengas g sal
h levántate

II   a iv b x   c xi d xii e i f v
g ii h vi i iii j ix k vii l viii

IV   a parece b vaya c beba
d coma e venga f fume
g haga h tome i acuéstese
j duerma

V   ¡hablen! ¡coman! ¡escriban!
sleep! go! come! go to bed!

VI   a gira/gire b sube/suba
c coge/coja d sigue/siga
e ve/vaya f mira/mire
g cruza/cruce h coge/coja
i baja/baje j mánda(me)/mánde(me)

VII   a precalenta b pica c bate
d mete e añade f mezcla
g calenta h vierte i fríe

VIII   a pase b coma c beba
d haga e cierre f abra
g presente h hable i venga

IX   a entrad   b formad   c buscad
d corred   e quedaos   f estirad
g haced   h bajad   i doblad
j descansad

X   a salgan   b giren   c cojan
d continúen   e crucen   f sigan
g tuerzan

XI   a ix b vii c v d i e viii
f x g iv h iii i ii j xi k vi

1.4

I   a pret b pret c pret d imp
e pret f imp g imp h imp
i pret j imp

1.4.1

I   a he b has c ha d han
e han f hemos g habéis h ha
i ha j hemos

II   a hemos b han c ha d ha
e habéis f han g has h he
i ha j ha

1.4.2

I   a jugado b comido
c terminado d vendido
e escuchado f perdido
g escogido h esperado
i organizado j invitado
k lavado l pedido m cerrado
n empujado o tirado p olvidado
q salido r entrado s oído
t partido

II   a jugado b tomado
c llamado d hablado
e asegurado f decidido
g enviado h cambiado
i imprimido j mirado

III   a visto b escrito
c puesto d hecho e dicho
f vuelto

IV   ha + a ganado b querido
c visto d comprado e gustado,

decidido   **f** puesto   **g** hecho
h visto   **i** creído   **j** seguido
k excedido   **l** detenido   **m** tenido

V

a Sofía leído su última novela.
b ¿Has leído el libro?
c No hemos leído el libro.
d Han visto la película del libro.
e Sofía ha visto la película ayer.
f Aún no hemos visto la película.
g Has/Ha/Habéis/Han visto la película?

1.4.3

I   **a** me he + levantado   **b** se ha
c se ha   **d** se ha   **e** se han
f te has   **g** nos hemos   **h** se han
i se han   **j** te has

1.4.5

I   **a** dormía   **b** miraba   **c** leía
d charlaba   **e** hablábamos
f duchaba   **g** telefoneaba
h reparaban   **i** jugaban

II   **a** era   **b** iban   **c** éramos
d eras   **e** iba

III   **a** esperaba   **b** escuchabas
c íbamos   **d** leía   **e** esperaba
f salía   **g** estaban   **h** hacía   **i** veíais
j bebía

IV   **a** hacía   **b** nevaba   **c** hacía
d soplaba   **e** brillaba   **f** llovía
g desaparecía   **h** hacía   **i** había
j estaba

V   **a** era, vivía   **b** estaban   **c** había
d cultivaba   **e** trabajaban
f recogían   **g** hacían   **h** había
i cocinaba   **j** tenía   **k** tardaba

VI   **a** me levantaba   **b** me duchaba
c me vestía   **d** me lavaba   **e** me
miraba   **f** se levantaba   **g** se
duchaba   **h** se vestía   **i** nos
dábamos   **j** se despertaban   **k** se
enfadaban   **l** se paseaba

1.4.7

I   **a** hablé   **b** hablaste   **c** habló
d hablaron   **e** comieron
f comimos   **g** ¿comisteis?   **h** vivió
i vivió   **j** vivimos

II   **a** charlé   **b** tomé   **c** llamé
d hablamos   **e** aseguró
f decidimos   **g** envió   **h** cambié
i imprimí   **j** miré

III   **a** jugué   **b** crucé   **c** busqué
d buscamos   **e** cruzamos
f buscaron   **g** jugó   **h** jugaron

IV   **a** dio   **b** dieron   **c** fuimos
d fui   **e** fue   **f** vi   **g** fui
h vimos

V   **1** fuimos   **2** quedamos
3 alquilamos   **4** hizo   **5** pasé
6 vinieron   **7** divertimos
8 cenamos   **9** bailamos
10 hicimos   **11** fuisteis
12 hicisteis

VI   **a** nos despertamos   **b** nos
levantamos   **c** nos paseamos
d nos equivocamos   **e** nos
perdimos   **f** nos paramos
g se puso   **h** se acordó
i se fue

1.4.9

I   **a** vivían, nació   **b** era, se mudó
c tenía, nació   **d** sufrió, tenía
e cruzaba, se paró   **f** vio, esperaba
g tenía, pasó   **h** estudiaba, decidió
i hacía, vio   **j** trabajaba, conoció
k era, solicitó   **l** hacía, se casaron

1.5.1

I   **a** voy   **b** vas   **c** va   **d** va
e vamos   **f** vais   **g** van   **h** van
i van   **j** voy

II   **a** van   **b** va   **c** va   **d** van   **e** va
f va   **g** va   **h** vamos   **i** va   **j** vais

1.5.2

I **a** miraremos **b** prepararás
c meteréis **d** comerán
e permitirá **f** escribirá **g** llegarán
h entraremos **i** partiré **j** subirán

II **a** llevaré **b** llevará **c** llevará
d llevará **e** llevarán **f** llevarán
g llevaremos **h** llevará **i** llevarás

III **a** tendré **b** vendréis **c** harás
d habremos **e** saldrá **f** sabrá
g querrán **h** diremos **i** pondréis
j podrán **k** tendrá **l** vendré

IV **a** tendré **b** iré **c** haré
d enviaré **e** irás **f** vendrás,
iremos **g** podremos, será, costará
h volveré, trabajaré

V **a** saldremos **b** cogerán
c esperará, llevará **d** podrá
e comerán **f** podrán **g** hará,
tendrán

1.5.3

VI **a** comería **b** bebería
c dormiría **d** hablaría **e** viviría
f compraría **g** pediría
h escucharía **i** miraría

VII **a** jugaría **b** jugaría **c** jugarían
d jugaríamos **e** jugaríais

VIII **a** preferiría **b** preferiría
c preferirían **d** preferiríamos
e preferiría

IX **a** me gustaría **b** le apetecería
c le encantaría **d** les interesaría
e te apetecería **f** os gustaría **g** le
gustaría **h** les gustaría

X **a** haría **b** saldría **c** tendría
d diría **e** vendría **f** podría
g pondría **h** sabría **i** querría
j habría

XI **a** podría **b** podríamos
c podríamos **d** podría **e** podrías

f podría **g** podrían **h** podríamos
i podríamos **j** podríamos

1.6.3

I **a** venir **b** coger **c** hacer
d sentirse **e** estar **f** tener
g saber **h** poder **i** tener
j querer

1.8.2

I

a Tengo dolor de cabeza.
b ¿Tienes dolor de los dientes?
c Le duele el pie.
d Me duelen los brazos.
e Le duele la rodilla.
f ¿Tiene usted dolor de cabeza?
g Tiene dolor de oídos.
h ¿Tenéis dolor de ojos?
i ¿Les duele la espalda?
j Le duele la espalda.

II **a** tenemos razón **b** no tienes
razón **c** tengo calor **d** tiene sed
e tienen hambre **f** tenemos frío
g tengo sed **h** usted tiene mucho
sueño **i** tenemos suerte **j** tengo
prisa **k** no tienen razón **l** tengo
mucho frío **m** tienen calor
n tenemos sed **o** tengo miedo de
las arañas **p** ¿tienes sed? **q** ¿tiene
frío? **r** ¿tenéis ganas de comer?
s ¿tienen hambre? **t** ¿tienes razón?
u ¡no tiene razón! **v** ¿tenéis
miedo? **w** no tengo miedo **x** no
tiene miedo **y** tenemos que irnos
z siempre tiene razón

1.8.3

I **a** hay, hay **b** hay, hay **c** había
d había, hay **e** había

1.8.4

I **a** conozco **b** conoce **c** saben
d conocemos **e** conoce
f conocen **g** conocen **h** sabemos
i saben **j** sabe **k** sé

1.8.7

I **a** Me acuerdo de John. **b** El se acuerda de mí. **c** Se acuerda de mi casa. **d** Recordamos nuestras vacaciones. **e** Me acuerdo de su mujer. **f** Recuerdo su sonrisa. **g** Mis niños se acuerdan de ella.

1.8.8

I **a** Yo no fui nunca a España. **b** EIlos no hicieron daño a nadie. **c** No veo nunca a Alicia./Nunca veo a Alicia. **d** No tienen nada en su casa. **e** ¿No aprendiste nunca a nadar? **f** Yo no veo a nadie. **g** Ella no monta nunca en bicicleta. **h** No tengo nada en mi bolsillo. **i** Nunca he ido a Mallorca. **j** Nadie está en casa.

II **a** iv **b** vi **c** i **d** ii **e** v **f** iii

1.8.9

I **a** dónde **b** cómo **c** cuándo **d** por qué **e** qué **f** cuándo **g** cuántos **h** a quién

1.8.10

I **a** Vivo aquí desde hace ... **b** Aprendo el español desde hace ... **c** Conozco a mi mejor amigo/a desde hace ...

II **a** acaba **b** acaba **c** acabamos **d** acaban **e** acabo

2

sister, restaurant, market, morning, vegetables, soup, lunch, dishes, night, fridge

2.2

I **a** el **b** la **c** el **d** el **e** la **f** el **g** la **h** la **i** el **j** el **k** el

II **a** la **b** la **c** la **d** la **e** la **f** el **g** la **h** el **i** la **j** el

III

a el **b** el **c** el **d** el **e** la **f** la **g** el **h** el **i** la **j** la **k** el **l** el **m** el **n** el **o** el **p** la **q** la **r** la **s** la **t** el

2.3.1

I **a** los peces **b** los gatos **c** los barcos **d** las terrazas **e** los padres **f** las moscas **g** los castillos **h** los alemanes **i** los españoles

2.4

I **a** un **b** una **c** un **d** una **e** un **f** una **g** un **h** una **i** una **j** un

2.4.1

I **a** Juan es bailador. **b** Rodríguez es estudiante. **c** Ramón es cantante. **d** Enrique es actor. **e** Estrellita es católica. **f** Pilar es empleada. **g** Es automovilista.

2.5

I **a** la **b** la **c** el **d** la **e** la **f** el **g** la **h** el **i** la **j** el **k** la **l** la **m** la **n** la **o** el **p** el **q** la **r** el **s** la **t** la

2.6.1

I **a** mis **b** mi **c** mi **d** mis **e** mis **f** mi **g** mis **h** mi **i** mis **j** mi

II **a** mi **b** mi **c** mi **d** mis **e** mis **f** mi **g** mi **h** mi **i** mis **j** mi

III **a** mis **b** mi **c** mi **d** mi **e** mi **f** mi **g** mis **h** mis **i** mi **j** mi **k** mis

2.6.2

I **a** tus **b** tu **c** tu **d** tus **e** tu **f** tus **g** tu **h** tus **i** tus **j** tu

II **a** tus **b** tu **c** tu **d** tus **e** tus **f** tu **g** tu **h** tus **i** tus **j** tus

2.6.3

I **a** sus **b** su **c** su **d** su **e** su
f sus **g** su **h** su **i** sus **j** su

II **a** su **b** su **c** sus **d** su **e** sus
f su **g** su **h** sus **i** su **j** sus

2.6.4

I **a** nuestra **b** nuestro
c nuestros **d** nuestra **e** nuestros
f nuestro **g** nuestro **h** nuestro
i nuestro **j** nuestros

2.6.5

I **a** vuestra **b** vuestra **c** vuestro
d vuestros **e** vuestro **f** vuestros
g vuestro **h** vuestros **i** vuestra
j vuestras

2.6.6

I **a** su **b** su **c** sus **d** su **e** sus
f sus **g** su **h** su **i** sus **j** su

2.6.7

I **a** su **b** su **c** sus **d** sus **e** su
f sus **g** sus **h** su **i** su **j** sus

2.7.1

I **a** este **b** esta **c** este **d** estas
e estos

2.7.2

I **a** aquel **b** aquella **c** aquellos
d aquel **e** aquel

2.7.3

I **a** cuánto **b** cuántas **c** cuánto
d cuántos

3.1.8

I **a** yo **b** nosotros/nosotras
c ellas **d** ellos **e** él **f** ella **g** tú/
usted/vosotros/vosotras/ustedes

II **a** él **b** ellos **c** yo **d** usted
e nosotros **f** ellas **g** ella **h** ellos
i tú **j** él

3.2

I **a** new car **b** it **c** a cat
d a tree **e** the wing mirror
f a bunch of flowers **g** the car

3.2.1

I **a** las **b** la **c** la **d** la **e** la
f la **g** los **h** los **i** la

3.2.2

I **a** te **b** me **c** os **d** nos
(visitarnos)

3.2.3

I **a** me **b** os **c** te **d** nos

3.3

I **a** me **b** her **c** me **d** him
e me **f** her **g** me **h** him **i** her
j him **k** her **l** me **m** me

3.3.1

I te, me, nos, te, le, les, os, le

3.3.2

I **a** me los/las **b** mándeselo/la
c se lo **d** dártelos/dárselas, etc.
e contárselo

3.3.3

I **a** me lo/la **b** quitárselo/la
c nos los/las **d** explicárselo
e pónganselos

3.4

I **a** él **b** ella **c** ellas **d** usted
e ti **f** vosotras **g** ustedes **h** mí
i nosotros

3.4.1

I **a** ¡míranos! **b** ¡mírale!
c ¡míralas! **d** ¡mírala! **e** ¡mírame!

3.5.1

I **a** ¡Lavaos! **b** ¡Lávese!
c ¡Lávate!

3.6

I **a** cuántas **b** cuánta **c** cuántos
d cuánto **e** cuántas

3.7

I **a** la mía **b** los míos **c** el mío
d las mías **e** mías **f** mía **g** míos
h mío

II **a** las suyas **b** el suyo **c** los
suyos **d** la suya **e** suyo **f** suya
g suyos **h** suyas

III **a** los vuestros **b** el vuestro
c la vuestra **d** las vuestras
e vuestros **f** vuestra **g** vuestras
h vuestro

3.8.4

I **a** a quien/a la cual **b** que **c** a
quien(es) **d** cuyo **e** quien **f** que

3.9

I **a** éste **b** éstas **c** éste **d** ésta
e éste **f** ésta **g** éstos **h** éste
i éstos **j** éstos

II **a** ésas/aquéllas **b** ésa/aquélla
c ésas/aquéllas **d** ése/aquél
e ésos/aquéllos **f** ése/aquél
g ésa/aquélla **h** ése/aquél
i ésa/aquélla **j** ésos/aquéllos

4

I **a** short, fat **b** long, blond, green
c new **d** new, casual **e** large, old
f tall, dark **g** small **h** older,
younger **i** favourite **j** cold

4.1

I
a nuevo/antiguo
b nueva/antigua
c nuevos/antiguos
d nuevas/antiguas
e nuevo/antiguo
f nueva/antigua
g nuevos/antiguos
h nuevas/antiguas

4.1.4

I **d** grande **e** débil
g inteligentes **i** guapa **j** fáciles
m mala **n** jóvenes **p** delgada
q trabajadores **t** amistosos

II **a** gordo **b** gorda **c** holgazana
d buenos **e** trabajador
f trabajadora **g** buenas **h** buenos
i natural **j** naturales **k** vieja
l viejo **m** Bajos **n** baja **o** nueva
p nuevo **q** nuevos, caros **r** ancha
s grande **t** buenas

4.1.5

I **a** alemán **b** inglés
c americana **d** español
e españoles **f** ingleses **g** italiano
h americanos **i** escocés
j canadienses

4.1.6

I **a** roja **b** marrones **c** verde
d azul **e** naranja **f** blancos
g violeta **h** amarillas **i** negro
j grises **k** rosada

4.1.7

I **a** mal **b** primer **c** San
d gran **e** gran **f** ninguna
g buen **h** cien **i** tercer **j** algún

4.4.1

I **a** más rápido **b** más guapa
c más grandes **d** más interesantes

e más difícil   **f** más hermosa
g más cara   **h** más pobres   **i** un
collar más precioso   **j** una bicicleta
más bonita

II   **a** más   **b** más   **c** menos
d más   **e** menos   **f** más   **g** más
h más   **i** menos   **j** más

4.4.2

I   **a** más   **b** más   **c** más   **d** el más
e las más   **f** más   **g** la más   **h** las
más

II   **a** más alta   **b** más largo   **c** más
seca   **d** la más lluviosa   **e** más
industrializada   **f** la más famosa
g más interesantes   **h** más
conocido   **i** más guapa   **j** más
antigua

4.4.3

I   **a** tan grande como   **b** más
grande que   **c** menos grande que
d menos grandes que
e menos grande que   **f** más
grandes que

II   **a** más alto que   **b** menos largo
que   **c** más caluroso que   **d** tan
hermoso como   **e** más agotadora
que

4.4.4

I   **a** mejor   **b** mejores   **c** mejor
d mejores   **e** mejor   **f** mejores

II   **a** el mejor   **b** los mejores
c las mejores   **d** la mejor   **e** la
mejor   **f** los mejores   **g** la mejor
h el mejor

5.1.1

I   **a** secamente   **b** locamente
c sencillamente   **d** rápidamente
e enormemente   **f** sinceramente
g raramente   **h** felizmente
i verdaderamente   **j** seriamente

5.3

I   **a** lentamente (despacio)
b completamente   **c** estrictamente
d demasiado   **e** fuerte(mente)
(alto)

6.2.10

I   **a** a la   **b** al   **c** a la   **d** al   **e** al
f a la   **g** al   **h** a la   **i** al   **j** al

II   **a** de   **b** de   **c** de las   **d** del
e del   **f** de   **g** de   **h** de los   **i** de
j de

III   **a** al, con   **b** en   **c** con   **d** a la
e enfrente del   **f** después de, a la
g con   **h** hasta